# TREASURE AND SCAVENGER HUNTS

## How to Plan, Create, and Give Them

(Second, updated edition)

## *Other Books by Gordon Burgett*

How to Create Your Own Super Second Life: What Are You
 Going to Do With Your Extra 30 Years?
Sell and Resell Your Magazine Articles
Publishing to Niche Markets
Standard Marketing Procedures for All Dentists (*with Reece
 Franklin*)
Niche Marketing for Writers, Speakers, and Entrepreneurs
Writer's Guide to Query and Cover Letters
The Travel Writer's Guide
How to Sell More Than 75% of Your Freelance Writing
Self-Publishing to Tightly-Targeted Markets
Empire-Building by Writing and Speaking
Speaking for Money! (*with Mike Frank*)
Query Letters/Cover Letters: How They Sell Your Writing
How to Sell 75% of Your Freelance Writing
Ten Sales from One Article Idea
The Query Book

# TREASURE

## and

# SCAVENGER
## HUNTS

## How to Plan, Create, and Give Them

## Second, updated edition

### Gordon Burgett

# Treasure and Scavenger Hunts.
## How to Plan, Create, and Give Them

**Cover by Anthony Avila**
**Inside artwork by Brandon Carr**

ISBN 0-9708621-7-2

# Table of Contents

# PART III

## The Super Party

# DEDICATION

To my mother, Lois Thelma Burgett, who died when the earlier edition of this book was in its gestation stage. I'm the first product of her first gestation stage, and much of the humor on these pages came from her. If you don't see any humor on these pages, you're lucky she's gone. She'd have chased you, sat on you, then made you laugh!

*and*

A favorite employee of days gone by, Jose Bookmyer, who was neither Hispanic nor male but a wise, sweet, droll Scottish lass who was a terror to my debtors but a joy to me. She promised to save me a celestial seat. Perhaps she has even befriended my mother. A couple more updatings of this book and I'll be joining you. (Having a much-frocked minister for a twin brother has to count for something.)

# ACKNOWLEDGMENTS

The clue in German was translated by Ms. Bianca Rosenthal; that in Italian, by Ms. Gina Glass. Thanks to Ray and Virginia Imig, witnesses of my misspent youth, who first exposed me to a big-time treasure hunt. And to a score of other friends in Illinois, Arizona, California, and South America who served as amiable guinea pigs, racing around town and otherwise inconveniencing innocent people at my behest while I learned my trade.

# Introduction

Treasure and scavenger hunts aren't nuclear physics nor do they lead to the salvation of peoplekind, but done right they can be plenty of fun and create a joyous core of an unforgettable gathering that can lighten, for a few hours, the otherwise more ponderous problems facing us and our kin.

Cavefolk didn't have treasure hunts for fun. They ate whatever treasure they could catch, and scavenged for the rest. No treasure, end of the game! The Dark Agers didn't have it much better. Even when the sun shone—yes, there was sun in the Dark Ages—they spent far too much time not being somebody else's treasure.

But we've got it easier: pizza, VCR's, penicillin, cars, even the wherewithal and place to have parties. Good thing I waited until now to write this book!

(There's even more in this second, revised edition. New tools, mainly. Now we can hunt without leaving our chairs: on the website. Even more exciting, we can capture the clues on a digital camera, then show the results at the party later, with nature still intact.)

Whatever implements or guile required, we're only going to live once (at least where I live), so why not have some fun along the way? Better yet, some challenging fun, the kind that calls into play your feet, mind, memory, wit, and cunning? A good treasure/scavenger hunt does all of that.

This book tells how.

# Additional Introduction
## for the Second Edition

When I wrote the first edition of this book some seven years back, I hadn't expected it to be so popular nor to hear from so many users over such a long period of time. That edition had to be reprinted regularly, but each time I left the text just as it was. It seemed to be what the buyers or party-givers needed or ordered, so why alter or amend what was working?

Oh yes, some told me of the ways they modified the book's suggestions (many were extraordinarily clever, some botched it up royally) but that's the book's purpose anyway, to provide a how-to framework to be adjusted to fit 100 uses and sizes.

Then a new century crept in and with it came a cascade of new tools and electronic gadgets. So I was compelled to rethink whether it wasn't time to carefully reread the earlier book, update the references (though I had mostly avoided citing medieval contemporaries in the first version), and see just how much better the whole treasure and scavenger hunting process would be by incorporating current doodads.

This book is the result. It is about 98% unchanged. Not because I couldn't let go of divinely-inscribed words nor because it was a work of art that would crumble if altered But because the gist of the game is far more mental than physical—it's a mind game that also involves the other senses (and cars, the clock, and pencils)—and as much as I tried, I could find only a few places where electronics added much to cunning.

There is a short chapter called "Twenty-first Century Tools" in which I suggest ways that the Internet (and, by assumption, computers) and digital cameras might add new dimensions to the basic hunts and party.

And every now and then I updated scavenger items and tweaked the processes.

Mostly I made the prose clearer.

The book works as well today as it did in 1994 or the years in between. Treasure and scavenger hunts can still be the heart of a great, fun party for players of any age. I focus mostly on adults in this book, and send you to other good books for kids, although the process for smaller players is but a pinch different than that described. Clever minds need go no farther than this book to find a workable core for youngsters and teens.

It's your party! Have fun!

# A BONUS TEASER!

**CRYPTIC CLUE**

11  5  5  16  /  20  8  9  19  /

2  15  15  11  / !

1  21  20  8  15  18  /

5  24  16  5  3  20  19  /

**Mysterious Item**

20  8  5  /

14  15  2  5  12  /  16  18  9  26  5  / .

3  1  18  20  15  15  14  9  19  20  /

20  15  15  / .

*(From cover artwork by Anthony Avila.)*

# PART I

## TREASURE HUNTS

# Treasure Hunts: What are they?

In the simplest terms, treasure hunts are a search for something of value. The search can be done individually: children scouring the yard for Easter eggs. Or collectively: four knee-knocking adults creeping through the woods or cemetery for a clue that will lead them to their next destination.

The treasure can be the direct reward of the search, like candy hidden in the den or a $5 bill under a rock in a cave. Or it can be tantalizingly wrapped and displayed on the sponsor's parlor table, to be awarded to the team with the highest point total.

It can be truly valuable, booty gathered during the hunt, or something more symbolic, like certificates of first place.

In other words, if treasure of any kind is involved and you have organized people to get it, you have a treasure hunt! You can title it, dress it however you wish, and direct it your way.

The harder part is planning and executing it so the players have fun, are challenged, and enjoy the search. The ideal is a treasure hunt that leaves them begging to take part again next year. The worst scenario has the participants in jail, hurt, or yawning in boredom.

This book helps you create the ideal.

# Who are Treasure Hunts for?

I suppose you could have a treasure hunt for anybody old enough or capable of grasping the concept who is able to seek the treasure. Children have them. So do the aged. In this book I will focus on adults, since their greater wisdom and mobility allow a greater intellectual and geographic challenge. But children will be addressed too, as will early teens. There is much overlap, in fact, so one can dip freely into one description for another age category.

Another aspect should be mentioned, though it is so close to common sense I beg you not to laugh at its suggestion.

Within every age category there are people or groups with limitations, and when catering to them as a unit your hunt must be trimmed to meet those limitations.

If the participants are wheelchair bound, clues fiendishly stuffed into the eaves of the attic or enticingly tied to the top branches will be cruelly out of reach. They can be no less ingeniously concealed at lower levels.

Likewise, those for whom reading is almost out of reach should not be baited with clever wordplay nor should the truly uncoordinated be asked to thread needles. You get the idea. Match the concept and clues to the doable fun zone of the players.

# Treasure Hunts for Kids

First, who are "kids" in this context? Little people after they can walk, much bigger people in their early teens, plus anybody in between.

My experience with this age group has been at Easter when I hid jelly beans in a room of our house, then released my daughters to gather as much booty as they could grab. Not too sophisticated, all clues visual (once they had lifted, shaken, or probed anything unattached), no instructions other than limiting the amount of plunder they could eat.  Ten minutes to buy the candy, ten minutes to hide it, and about four minutes of supervision so they didn't whack the chandelier with the broom or otherwise destroy the fixtures. Fast, cheap fun—and a family Easter tradition.

That summarizes most of the treasure hunts one has for younger kids.

They are simple, the kids seek the actual prizes themselves, those prizes are usually edible, and since the hunters' attention spans are very short, so are the hunts.

The best book for kids is surely Lenny Hort's *Treasure Hunts! Treasure Hunts!* (HarperCollins, 2000), an 80-page fortune chest full of adventure and common sense. The hunts include hidden objects (like coins, peanuts, and ice), clues, mazes, even the Internet. He also explains car and bus hunts while the waifs are captive passengers.

Properly, many of the treasure hunts have scavenger components as well, both in the yard and the house. Hort does for kids what we do for adults, with plenty of examples, set-up advice, and some actual starting clues and scavenger lists.

Deanna Cook, in her *Family Fun's Parties* (Hyperion, 1999), tells of a fairly typical Easter Egg Hunt where the players are divided into two groups, the toddlers in the front yard and the older kids, in the back. There are two kinds of eggs. Plastic eggs, filled with small toys, jelly beans, and wrapped candies, are scattered within reach of the hunters, in the bushes and low branches for easy gathering. The fancier plastic eggs, decorated with flair, are much harder to find (for example, in drain pipes or under piles of leaves). They are worth more too: a pick from the prize table where stuffed animals and chocolate bunnies wait enticingly.

Similar Easter games are found in *Great Parties for Kids* (Williamson, 1994), by Nancy Fyke, Lynn Nejam, and Vicki Overstreet, with the time limits an hour for those 4-7 and 90 minutes for the 8-10 group.

In one they fill the plastic eggs with store coupons—the store being a table of goodies the coupon-finders can rush to immediately or at the end of their hunting.

Another fairly recent source of fun activity for kids in Debra Wise's thick *The Reader's Digest Great Big Book of Children's Games* (Reader's Digest, 1999), with more than 450, including a few treasure and scavenger selections.

In *50 Fabulous Parties for Kids* (Crown, 1994), Linda Hetzer describes a treasure hunt for tikes 6-9, which she schedules after the kids have eaten, as a party-closer. In it, various clues are written on separate sheets of paper that are hidden throughout the house and yard, well out of view. Then she reads the first clue and they all guess, then scurry to that site to see if they were right. If so, she reads the second (of 6-8 clues) ... When they find the last clue, everybody wins equal prizes!

Linda also suggests that the Treasure Boxes of party prizes, at the solution site to the last clue, be hidden in a closet or a bathtub with the curtain closed, so they wouldn't be found too early. That would have worked a Bronx minute in our house (even though the bathtub was usually a place to be avoided). Where prizes were concerned, at least my kids could outsmell bloodhounds! Maybe the car trunk in the garage...

Deanna Cook best describes the rule-writing process and guidelines needed when youngsters are involved. In describing her "Ultimate Treasure Hunt," she suggests tying all of the clues and décor to the party theme (hers include a puppy party, a butterfly party, a miniature party, and a pirate party), starting in reverse by hiding the treasure first, writing a clue for that spot, then doing the clues from last to first, making certain to find clever hiding spots and keeping the clues to the level of the hunters. The clues can be riddles, drawings, coded messages, maps... (There's a chapter about clue writing later in this book too.) Make sure that the boundaries are clearly defined, particularly outdoors, that the cluemaker keeps a master clue list where each is hidden, and that everybody who takes part gets some kind of prize.

Her "Puppy Party," in *Family Fun's Parties*, would be great for the youngest buccaneers. In it you hide about 40 cardboard bones, all about doggy high. The kids must hunt on their hands and knees, gathering bones to put in their own pile, to be swapped later for prizes.

Lenny Hort gives all the details for a "Magazine Hunt." Which is a great fallback if an outdoor party is rained out. What's needed is 12-15 old magazines and catalogs (the more photos in them, the better), scissors for everybody, and a master list, which can actually be composed by the participants before they open up the magazines. The list has 20 or so items that the player wants to find on the pages, as a photo, a drawing, even a toy or figure, just so it matches the listed item. Thirty minutes: the most items cut out wins.

What kinds of things might be on the list? *Treasure Hunts! Treasure Hunts!* includes a clown, caveman, submarine, school bus, volcano, lobster, the queen of England... He makes a super suggestion that as soon as a person cuts an item from the publication, it is put back into the center pile and they look through another. That way everybody has a shot at the more illustrative offerings.

Most of the books cited also describe scavenger hunts. Cook has two with particular appeal. One is a rainy day "Critter Hunt" where the goal is to gather up anything on the surface drawn up by the precipitation, like earthworms, salamanders, and frogs. Later, of course, they must be returned, unharmed. (Might do that *after* the Magazine Hunt!)

The other is simply the nature hunt, whether it's the Fall Scavenger Hunt (in quest of berries, cattails, mushrooms, and milkweed pods) or the Beach Scavenger Hunt (to find sand dollars, 10 pieces of trash, driftwood, or a polished stone).

There are two ways to do these, to minimize the cost to nature: one is to collect and then return all live items, the other is to find and have the rest of the team sign off that it was found, while also listing the location and every color on it.

There are many treasure hunts can be done in the car while crossing the veldt with a pack of wide-eyed get. Everyone is handed a list of things likely to be seen, like a goat, pear tree, barn, cow, motorcycle, corn, tractor, silo, train, cemetery, split rail fence, school, railroad station, hayfield, pond, wheat, apple tree, river, tomatoes, bicycle, and a rusted old car.

Then when an item on the list is seen, the person yells it out! First to yell gets credit for that item. The person with the most credits in, say, 30 minutes wins.

Or you can play that once an item is seen, that's it. (One credit per cow, not a credit every time a new cow is seen.) You make up the rules and decide if one person keeps score (a mother's job, usually) or each person keeps their own tally.

Alphabet is a variation: the first to find something outside the car that starts with an "A," then a "B," and so on...

You can mix it up by having the items stationary the first time through, moving the second, then animal, then vegetable, then mineral, and so on, inventing categories at will. Why stop with letters? Why not numbers? One house, two (but only two) trees, three parked trucks, four fence posts...

In an ancient book in the library, alas in a revised edition of *The Cokesbur Party Book* (Abingdon Press, 1959), Arthur M. Depew suggested several fun ways to test the sensory hunting skills of kids (or teens).

In one, participants are blindfolded and led to smell various items—an onion, tobacco, cheese, fish, French fry, beer—to see if they can identify the objects. They could do this one at a time, with the others outside the room. Or, for more fun, let in as teams, holding hands, to smell each item as a group, then quietly decide (without the others hearing them) what it is, while other teams are doing the same with other items.

A variation might have the players all facing one direction, grouped as teams, while the host drops an item behind them. They will huddle and guess what it was, writing the answer on a sheet of paper. Depew suggests dropping things like a shoe, ball, book, beanbag, sponge, pencil, knife, and a coin.

Another variation, probably best done individually, is to blindfold kids and have them guess what various objects are by feel: raw liver, egg, oyster, asparagus stalk, cheese ball, used bow resin, play dough, calf tongue....

By far the most elaborate example I've found in print appears in Meredith Brokaw and Annie Gilbar's excellent *The Penny Whistle Party Planner* (Fireside, 1991) in which a "Pirate Treasure Hunt Party" for ages four and up is described. Each of the five steps of organization, planning, and implementation are fully explained. Included is sending an invitation in invisible ink while gathering up lots of junk jewelry, finding and buying gold items (coins, candy, foil), and laying in a stock of bandannas, eye patches, pirate hats, and cork (blackened later to make mustaches on the participants).

Many of the details refer to creating the proper atmosphere for an outdoor (front and back yard) or indoor hunt, depending on the weather, as well as the proper music, food, and table setting.

Each child makes their own treasure chest from small gift boxes you provide upon which they glue beads, sequins, wrapping paper, lace, press-on letters, whatever else you put at their disposal. All the bounty they gather at the party goes into their own box, which they take home with the bandanna, eye patch, and hat!

The games that Brokaw and Gilbar suggest include making the treasure hunt boxes; "Blind Man's Bluff" using a treasure map and a crayon, closest to the treasure with their mark wins; "Musical Chairs," to the music of a pirate song, and "Captain Hook's Crocodile Hunt," where hunters seek out a loud alarm clock before the alarm goes off.

The actual form of the hunt depends upon the age of the hunters. For those 5-8, they suggest a "Picture Treasure Hunt" where the youngsters seek out pictures from a magazine (or elsewhere) of the items they actually win, and are given afterwards or at lunch. For older children, they suggest a sequential clue hunt, all clues in poetry.

A wise observation is that with children nobody goes home without some kind of prize. Either you must help those less likely or able to find something or set a limit on the number of prizes any child can win, so there are enough to go around.

The "Pirate Treasure Hunt Party" is but one of 23 well explained parties for children in *The Penny Whistle Party Planner*. It includes a hundred ideas that can quickly be converted into parties for early teens and adults.

Incidentally, there are many books in The Penny Whistle series with activities for children that include hunts of all kinds.

The variety of hunts is as wide as your imagination. The trick is to hide something appropriate to the season, like eggs for Easter, green candies or paper shamrocks for St. Patrick's Day, whiskers for Ground Hog Day, bark for Arbor Day, paper gobblers for Thanksgiving, hearts at St. Valentine's Day. And remember that since the youngsters are seeking treasure, many like to do some actual digging. An old cigar box containing booty a few inches below the surface often satisfies this desire!

The leaf hunt in the fall is a perfect example. You can give each team a kind of leaf and that's what they are to gather. Or they can hunt by color, by length, by number of points, by beauty...(Of course it's perfectly permissible for them to bring those leaves to one place, near a trashcan or garbage bag. Why be so subtle? Give out rakes and the tallest pile or the pile bagged quickest wins! The best idea? The team to fill the most bags in 15 minutes gets the biggest prizes!)

In another old gem gathering dust in your library (*Party Fun for Holidays and Special Occasions*, Harper, 1960), Margaret Mulac describes a "numbers hunt" that would work for somewhat older kids. Each team is looking for items that have that number on it, represent that number, or contain that particular number of things.

If ten items have been hidden or placed, inside or out, then the team must find those ten. The first team to find all ten wins—or at a certain time a bell is rung to call in the teams to reward those with the highest number found.

Number one might be represented by a one-cent stamp; two, a pair of eyeglasses; three, a clock with both hands stuck on three; four, a playing card with a four on it; five, five matches left in a book of matches; six, an empty six-bottle carton of soda pop; seven, a book with a marker at chapter seven; eight, a pack of gum with eight sticks left; nine, a glove or shoe size nine; ten, the letter "X" from a Scrabble set.

A variation of this is "Uncle Billy's House," presumably named for an old bachelor or widower who tried his hand at housekeeping. But he got things all wrong, which is what the hunters are looking for: things completely out of place in a regular home. Teams write down what they see in the house that simply doesn't fit, which you have scattered about earlier.

Let your imagination roam here. Be sure there are girls on each team. Some of the boys will not see the incongruities! Here are a few ideas:

(1) Shoes used as bookends
(2) A picture hanging sideways
(3) A tube of toothpaste with a toothpick sticking out of it
(4) The telephone book in the refrigerator
(5) The clock hours behind
(6) A seed packet in water in a clear vase
(7) Potatoes in the fruit bowl

(8) Newspapers inside the oven
(9) A picture of a gym shoe inside a frame
(10) A fork in the sugar bowl

Some of these ideas would work nearly as well for early teens or adults. And many of the adult ideas can be modified and simplified to work for children. The trick is to see the clues and tasks from the eyes of the doer, then lay out a hunt that matches their problem-solving capacity and their attention span.

# Treasure Hunts for Early Teens

Early teens are in limboland, wanting to do adult things but still bereft of much common sense, responsibility, or experience. New hormones have their bodies and faces in revolt. They're too young to drive and shouldn't be drinking. So parties for them (that aren't "stupid") are hard to plan.

Most of the boys would probably rather ride bikes, play ball, and pal around than go to a party, while most of the girls are ready to mix, dance, and act semi-"grown up." The word "jerk" too aptly applies, and "boy crazy" fits in too.

Therefore a treasure hunt is perfect: it forces them to mix, work as a unit, think, run, horse around, compete, and then come back to eat and act, again, like fools! The trick is to keep it all within foot distance of the home or gathering point, supervised, and so clear about the purpose, boundaries, and time limit that even the brain dead would understand!

Rather than devise a specific hunt for early teens, pluck from the Treasure Hunt for Adults, Scavenger Hunt for Adults, and the Super Party those things that match the early teens in question, plus your time and space limitations, and fashion a combo party that will work for them.

Still, here are some things to keep in mind:

(1) Theme parties work particularly well at this age. They give a reason for the gathering. If it's Halloween, for example, require them to wear costumes. At New Years, add in clues that refer to the year and what happened to them or at their school that was important during the past

year. Birthdays work in reverse: the party is the birthday person's gift to their friends!

(2) Party crashers can be a problem. If they will interfere if the group goes outdoors, limit the hunt to inside the guesthouse, or hold the gathering at a park where the supervisors can control outsiders at the gate, or even reconvene at a rural site where the teens are taken after first meeting at the host's house in town.

(3) A good way to eliminate or greatly reduce crashing is to have every participant bring one more person, but just one. You decide in advance if those "others" will be of the same sex or a "date." If they can't think of anyone or simply won't bring anyone, that's fine—but they must let you know at least a day ahead of time. That either includes or eliminates those most likely to crash.

(4) Be certain that the participants know how they should dress if much physical activity is involved, a lot of walking is required, or they need warm attire. Otherwise you can count on half of them being overdressed or underclad.

(5) Because hunts for early teens will be limited to at most the nearby blocks of a neighborhood, since the teams must walk, it's sensible to have a couple of supervisors or chaperones unobtrusively keep an eye on the hunters in that area, to see that others don't bother them, that they don't bother others, and that everything is running smoothly.

(6) If the prizes for the winning team(s) are popular items, tell what they are when you explain the rules. That will help keep squirrelly teen minds focused on the task at hand, and will give a reason for the other team members to keep the goof-offs in line!

(7) Everybody who takes part should get some kind of prize. However much they scoff at that prize, they'll put it in their pocket or purse and keep it. It's important at that age.

(8) Don't let the hunters change the rules or conditions before or during the game. Early teens love to challenge and change the best-laid plans. It's your hunt and you want to avoid confusion. Keep it simple and unchanged.

# Treasure Hunts for Adults

At last, the heart of this book. Treasure hunts for kids are fun, and for early teens, as fun as anything can be. But for adults (which, with a huge, tongue-in-cheek wink, includes later teens), they can be great, great fun!

To show you how much fun and how that is derived is the task of the remaining pages.

By extension, they can be just as much fun for the planner(s). Well done, they can make your party *the* party to attend, and eagerly anticipated year after year. They can brand you as some sort of genius—"who would have guessed?" And they can be one grande pain in the rump until they actually get together, "work," and the guinea pigs get back laughing, safe, and hungry.

The biggest drawback: you never get to take part. Worst yet, while teams are tromping through the woods or begging widows for a potato or shoe hook, you are left at camp zero to answer emergency phone calls, imagining cars full of friends flying off the bridge or your entire list of invitees in the holding tank unable—or too angry—to call!

Your only hope is that, inspired by your super party, a friend will try to do you one better, invite you to solve their clues, and they will be stuck alone with even greater misgivings!

Read on. Problems first, then an ideal treasure hunt, building solutions into the framework, and bringing it all together into a Super Party!

# Problems

When you invite 15 or 30 adults to a party, send them around town to find clues, set a return deadline to receive a prize, and none of them are angels to begin with, what do you get? Problems! You have two choices: forget about the treasure hunt or have it while trying to reduce the potential problems. If you choose the first, go find a whodunit to read: this book assumes you will select the second.

I see problems as falling into four rather vague categories: safety, time/space, clues, and matching. But don't limit your imagination solely to these four. Anything else you foresee must be treated in the same way: give it a name, describe the potential problem(s), and try to devise a way to eliminate or reduce it or them.

Let me describe these four areas briefly and express concerns in each. Later, when we discuss an actual model treasure hunt, I will try to include our solutions to each problem in the organizational framework.

# Problems with Safety

Put in the simplest terms, here are the safety concerns that immediately come to mind:

1. One of the invitees shows up under some foreign influence (like alcohol or drugs) and winds up as the team driver, with the obvious problems that could create.
2. Same situation, but this time the person simply goes berserk and imperils others and him or herself.
3. Somebody gets injured on the hunt, like when climbing in and out of the car, falling in a hole, or dropping dead from a stress-induced heart attack.
4. Somebody completely unrelated to your group causes injury or death to your invitees: a car crash or they are waylaid at Sixth and Pine by terrorists.
5. Someone not included in your group but knowledgeable about the hunt (like a jilted lover or vengeful ex-spouse) lays in wait to taunt the teams and shout obscenities.

Discouraged? Ready to play cards instead? Toughen up. You might also walk out your door and be instantly disintegrated by aliens, killed by invisible toxic fumes, or even gravitationally sucked downward several hundred feet where the stoop used to be. That's about as likely as the five concerns above ruining your party.

Still, let's look at each.

In the first case, it's hard to test the invitees for alcohol or other drugs in their system, but you can let the teams choose their own driver, if driving is involved. You can choose the drivers beforehand, based on what you know about their sobriety and driving safety or maturity. You can have the party in the daytime on Sunday (or Saturday) when foreign influences are less likely to be present. You can exclude fall-down drunks or other-orb druggies from your invite list. You can certainly ask in the invitation that the folks arrive sober because both a clear head and driving are required; partying will follow! Or you can, as the ultimate arbiter, directly intervene at the hunt if you see somebody driving that shouldn't be. Say something like, "This makes me nervous. Is there some other way we might handle the driving here?" The team will surely take the hint and someone else will volunteer.

The second case, a crazed lunatic cracking at the hunt, is far more alarming than likely, particularly if the steps in the preceding paragraph are taken. My best advice is to invite all crazed lunatics to somebody else's party the night you are holding yours. A party far, far away!

Somebody getting injured, case three, is harder to predict simply because people do get injured every day, some while they just stand still doing nothing. We'll discuss time/space as the next problem, which should help reduce this concern. Another way would be to make sure that every participant knows well in advance, perhaps in an explanation note accompanying or part of the invitation, just how much physical activity is required, how they should dress, and what they might do that could imperil them. Encourage those with personal health or safety concerns to call if they have any questions. Some may decide to help you fix food while the rest romp and leap.

You can't do much about the fourth case except to ask your hunters to not only take regular precautions with their driving, but to be extra careful since so many of your friends are in their hands. If you live in a war zone or terrorists are training on your street, wait for a better season to conduct your treasure hunt!

And the fifth case, the uninvited party crasher taunting and bedeviling your hunters. Don't invite anybody who is in that situation, if you know about it. And have an emergency phone number for all teams to call, if necessary. Should something like that occur and the team can't diplomatically defuse it at the time, they should call. Then you can either call the police or handle it yourself. Having said all that, I've never seen it happen nor heard of it, so I wouldn't worry unduly. The team might also be swept away by the Rapture. Or those people-disintegrating aliens....

It's nearly as much fun imagining pitfalls and solving them as it is writing clues!

There's a related problem, of a sort, that you're not likely to encounter, but on the long shot, let me share it.

My ex-wife and I once gave a treasure hunt on Halloween in Cartagena, Colombia, for local Peace Corps volunteers. We had planned to dispatch them around town in search of clues once they had arrived. It turned out that several of the guests were stopped somewhere en route to our place by the police and curtly informed that civilized people didn't walk around in masquerade. Moreover, it was against the law to be in public in a mask. After all, bank robbers and common thugs wore masks. So costumes came off, civvies went on, and so did the treasure hunt! The moral, I guess: forget costumes in public on Halloween in Cartagena, Colombia, but have a hunt anyway.

# Problems with Time and Space

Where you have the hunt and how long the participants have to complete the tasks can be problem-provoking. If the clue zone is 100 miles square and you give the teams 35 minutes to solve 10 clues, you have a potential death-inducer. On the other hand, if you confine the clues to a backyard and allow three hours, they might die from boredom. Somewhere in between you can keep them happy and healthy.

Regarding time, I've found 2-2.5 hours just about ideal, then I add on an additional 15 minutes bonus for them to get back safely. Three hours is probably the longest you can sustain interest unless the prizes are huge or the group is captive.

As you'll see later, I have so many things for the team to do in that time period they immediately realize that they can't do them all. Then it becomes a case of picking out the highest point-earning things, doing what they can, and seeing how they fare in total points. The effect is the reverse of what you imagine: it seems to reduce the inclination to drive 110 miles an hour and puts it on quality returns. It's less stressful.

As for space, keep the size of the driving area fairly small and give each team a map with the boundaries clearly marked. If the outside boundary is Main Street, be certain they understand whether both sides of Main are in play or just the side "inside" the clue zone. (I found it best to go one block beyond Main if clues were on both sides, then say everything "inside" the line on the map is in play.)

The terrain itself can be a concern. Unless warned, I don't imagine you want your guests wading in bayous or through the stockyard (and tracking that back to your rug—or the car interior). So tell them what they won't have to do or the kinds of terrain they won't have to cross, then don't plant items where that's even an issue.

If the median age of the hunters is 24, it shouldn't matter if the terrain is vertical, taxing, and requires short bounds over small creeks. But if the median age is 81, just getting around the house will be memorable, not to mention scaling stairs and curbs! Match the clue sites to the clue seekers.

Also, avoid "he-man" activities that will encourage the gents (and maybe some women) to climb trees, cross canyons hand-over-hand by cable, or check the underside of the local, passenger-ingesting Amtrak. I remember taking part in a hunt where we had to swing as high as the playground set would let us, with flashlight in hand, to glimpse a number written to be read only at the maximum peak of peril. The question was wimp, macho, or dead. Even the grandfathers were rushing to the swing to show that they still had it in them! Amazingly, all survived. Make the clues visible to the everyday crossword puzzle solver.

Finally, regarding space: keep the clues in places legally and sanely accessible at the hour of the hunt. If you put a clue on home plate on the local high school diamond to be found at night, see if that's not off bounds after dark. Under a spinster's front porch? On top of the town water tower? Inside a mailbox? Smarter thinking is required.

If you live in a small town, another step makes sense: let the police know what's up, that it'll only last a couple of hours, and if they have any questions, please call. They are glad to know, particularly if teens or young adults are concerned, and doubly so if they are in costume. Often they'll also help keep an eye on the hunters.

# Problems with Clues

Many of the clue-related problems come from the ways that treasure hunts are laid out.

The traditional way is that clue one, when solved, leads you to clue two, which, when solved, leads you to clue three, and so on. Let's call those sequential clues.

A basic problem with sequentialization is that when any clue is missing, returned to the wrong place, stolen, or simply blown away, all progress stops dead at that spot.

Other problems can come from the four ways sequential clues are laid out: (1) each team follows the same route in the same order; (2) each team follows the same route but they each start at a different clue; (3) each team has its own route and set of clues, or (4) some combination of (1)-(3), like three routes each followed by three teams starting at different clues.

ALRIGHT, MATEY! LAST CLUE SAYS TO DIG HERE!

The problem with (1) is that a smart team will just let a smarter team lead, playing follow-the-leader. When the leading team finds the last clue, they will tie them up or put them in a spell, solve that clue themselves, and rush away to claim the prize, hopefully eating or spending it before the other team returns to share their tale of woe! A bit dramatic, but you get the idea. Everybody is bunched up at the same places.

The second system partially solves that. Each team will start a clue apart and remain so, assuming they are equally brilliant or dense—an assumption that crumbles quickly as they, again, pile up at key clues.

That problem is solved with system (3). Yet it creates two huge problems of its own. One, the amount of work involved in creating and laying out three, five, or ten different sets of clues is overwhelming. Indeed, you are better off reading that whodunit. Plus the complaints later that "our clues were much harder than yours," or "our terrain was rougher," or "our drive was longer" aren't worth the hassle, because inevitably some will be harder, rougher, or longer.

The fourth system might solve some problems but it will inherit or create others.

By now you properly suspect that I'm not a fan of sequential clues. I'll show you a better way in a moment.

A very early treasure hunt that I laid out, at the outset of the Industrial Revolution, on the outskirts of Phoenix, Arizona, was done by the second system, sequential clues with teams starting at different points. The players were college friends, some Americans experienced at least with the concept, others from foreign lands where the idea of a treasure hunt meant about as much as a snipe hunt or Maypole scaling.

Alas, one team, chosen at random from a hat, was composed of four foreigners. I had my misgivings but they seemed bright and assured me that they understood precisely what they were to do. This hunt was held on foot in an area about a mile square, and the first team to bring back a numbered tag from each of the 10 sites would win. Off they went for what was limited to 90 minutes. I doubted anybody would get seven of the ten clues since they were so shrewdly worded and expertly placed. Twenty minutes later in bounded the foreigners, winded but clearly victorious! Until I looked at the tags. They had in fact solved their first two clues— and brought back all five tags, plus the clue, from each of the locations! They had the ten tags they thought they needed!

You can imagine the others' gripes when they went where they were certain the clue led them only to find an empty sack, without their tag or the next clue!

Plenty of cheap college food and beverage assuaged the rest of the players when they returned, and by the end of the night, after we had given away the prizes by playing other games, we all laughed at the snafu. But for me that was the end of sequential clues.

A second way, call it proliferation, is to give all the teams the same clues, let them find the sites, and collect whatever it is they are to gather to prove that they arrived.

That is far better. If a clue is too hard, they just go to the next one. If they can solve many or all of them at the outset, they can lay out their driving route to reap the maximum return in the least time and distance.

Most hunters, though, will solve the clues in the order in which they are written, and that can lead to bottlenecks and "follow-the-leader," so give everybody the same clues but list them in a different order. With cut-and-paste on a computer, even the old-fashioned rubber cement way, that is easy to do.

Another major change I make is not having anything removable at the clue site: no tags to bring back, no poker chips, nothing but a number that is well affixed for all time. The site might be a phone booth at Clark and Miner. The number is on the phone. They write that number by the clue, turn it in when they return, and if the number is right, bingo. It may be the branch number of a bank on the ATM machine, the capacity number in an elevator, the zip code of the town, or the price of a Mexican pizza at Taco Bell. I'll explain other ways this works later.

Since the team is seeking a number, if another team is tailing them they can quickly shake them with chicanery. Pull up to a light pole, all jump out, pretend to hunt for some number at the base, have one person write something down, and flee back to the car in mock jubilation. By the time the second group catches on, the first team is long gone. Even better if they find a number: the other team will be stumped for the rest of the night trying to match it to its proper clue!

Additional problems with clues?

1. Some people don't understand them.
2. They get stolen by outsiders who see hunters appear, take something, and hurry away. So they take something too—the clues—and run away!

Misunderstanding usually comes because hunters don't know what they must do once they get to the site to find the next clue: climb a tree, dig in the sand?

But if you know you are seeking a number, usually a specific number when there are many, that is what you must extract from the clue: where and, if an issue, which number. Granted, every team has one member who is lucky to find their car twice in a row. The rest of the team takes up the mental slack.

Soon enough we'll explain how clues are written so the confusion is further reduced.

As for stealing the clue(s), by the proliferation system there is nothing to steal. The number is affixed or part of the setting, like the phone number, the time on a clock, or the call numbers of a radio station. Poor thieves, they would be the most confused souls in the county. Like trying to steal the laugh from a joke.

# Problems with Matching

Matching refers to team formation.

One team has no driver, or at least none that should be let near a moving vehicle.

Another has two nonstop smokers, a Christian Scientist, and a Mormon.

Another, Ellie May Crasp, who nobody with a functioning nose wants to be near; Billy Barntop, who spits when he speaks, which is always; Ruth Ann Rollup, who can't hear a tornado, even repeated, and Axel Allright, who is certifiably daft. They refuse to leave the house in each other's company, and are only in the house at all as a favor to you.

There might be worse problems, but let's stick to the three biggest complaints: the driver, smoking, and other people.

If driving isn't involved, we just cured problem #1. If it is, one way is to ask, when people arrive, who would be willing to drive. Write their names on a sheet of paper, then pick those who appear to be sober, sane, and a reasonable bet on the freeway. (Would you let your mother-in-law in a car with them? Well, your daughter?) Make the drivers the team captains. That should eliminate the worst.

What if a person still refuses to go with a particular driver? Three choices:

(1) Ask them, if that driver promises to drive slowly and with care, would they go? If they say yes, talk with the driver, half-kiddingly. Something like, "Jimmy, every member of your team is petrified to ride with you! Will you keep

it slow and safe, or should I pick another driver?" Smile, they'll promise or refuse, and you make the decision.

(2) You switch the person to another team and put a less timorous (or dumber) soul with the driver-captain in question.

(3) Send out the team without that person, if they'd rather stay at the house. Have that person staying behind make the coffee or set the table: use your captive labor!

Smoking is a real issue. Even though the smokers may not smoke while the car is in motion, their cars often stink, and they'll exude the fumes from the quick hits they'll take while clue hunting.

On the other hand, some folks may just love the odor and think only wimps avoid secondhand smoke.

So it probably makes sense to ask the hunters, again, soon after arrival if smoking during the treasure hunt is an issue with them or if they prefer a smoke-free car. You have to ask the drivers if they smoke too, if you don't know. And then match the strong anti-smokers with each other.

As for the four souls who refuse to be matched with each other, you have two choices here. The first is not to invite them, which can be hard if they live in your house, employ you, or they married your kid. The second is to split them up ahead of time, if you know their peeves or traits. That is, let every team have one of them!

When it comes to creating teams, I'm very nervous with the usual system, which is to have everybody dip in and pull something out which, when matched, makes a team. For example, if there are four teams with four members each, you separate the face cards and aces, put them in a hat, and all who choose jacks go together.

I prefer to mix the sexes, a couple of each per four-person team, if possible. If there are a few teens and the rest are considerably older, why not put a teen on each team—or if there are just four, two couples, and they seem sensible about driving, have an all-teen team? It also seems prudent to have at least one person familiar with the terrain in each group; segregate the smokers, if that's an issue; keep Randy Retch away from his ex-wife and her wary boyfriend; make sure each team has a responsible driver, and try not to put four together whose combined IQ won't reach three digits.

That suggests that I simply pick the teams rather than leaving selection to fate. I'd rather they be a bit irked at me later for "putting them on a team with that idiot Igor" than having everybody gripe because none of the teams blended well.

# An Ideal Treasure Hunt

For me, an ideal treasure hunt must be fun and safe. Everything else is secondary.

There must be some prize, some reward for having toiled for several hours, even though it was fun toil. Something to lift in the air, kiss, and brandish with tales of heroism and idiocy for the rest of the party.

There must be some competition, some team purpose to cement the bonding needed to work as a unit. The greater the prize, the greater the motivation and bonding.

And it must be doable. The clues must be solvable. The sites must be findable. The teams must be able to amass enough things or points to look intelligent and productive.

I like to frame the hunt with a party. A short gathering first, for soft drinks and finger food. The hunt. And a food and a reasonable drinkfest following, with noise, prizes, jibing, flaunting, perhaps a few more games, and probably dancing. Something should follow that's as much fun as the hunt itself.

You want it to be an activity they won't forget. A good gauge: if, at the end, they don't ask when you're having another treasure hunt, something needs adjustment.

All that remains is to unveil the details: setting up the timetable, creating a framework, writing clues, and putting together a super party.

Except for one critical component: the scavenger hunt. A super party includes both wrapped into one!

So let's discuss a scavenger hunt in the same general way that we have a treasure hunt, then get to those details. (If we don't do it fast, forget it. I'm headed straight for the food table!)

# What are Scavenger Hunts?

Literally, to "scavenge" is to clean up (streets, alleys, etc.), to remove rubbish, dirt, and garbage, while a "scavenger" is an animal that eats garbage and decaying organic matter.

Fat chance you'll have people banging on your door to take part in that hunt!

Alas, the *Webster's New World Dictionary* to the rescue! A "scavenger hunt" is "a game, as at a party, in which persons are sent out to bring back a number of prescribed items without buying them."

That's just about it. Except I like to expand the usual "what can we get from the neighbors?" concept to include items of nature and things created or learned by the team before they return, to reduce the element of chance, to mix mental with physical activity, and to get everybody involved every moment that the hunt is on.

One of my daughters took this to an extreme many years back. She and her girlfriends, junior high school age, decided to fix dinner for one of the girl's working mother—plus themselves, of course. But the larder wasn't filled, and their purses were emptier yet. The item in question was potatoes, without which the meal would be incomplete. So she drew up three lists of scavenger items, most of them impossible (like a Will Rogers autograph or a red frog). Prominent, however, was one item very possible: a potato. As soon as each team collected a pair of potatoes, the hunt was over and supper was on!

Usually scavenger hunts are for fun, a match of wits and energy against other teams likewise employed. The items gathered have little or no pecuniary value.

Some things that should be excluded: items that must be returned (unless the team itself agrees to do that), anything living that won't be restored unharmed to nature, anything that requires permanently damaging the ecology (like having to pick live flowers, saw off limbs, or trample gardens), anything dangerous to the hunters, and anything that puts the group in harm's way (like having to go to a high crime area or climb a tree that extends over a canyon).

# Scavenger Hunts for Kids and Early Teens

Since nobody in either category drives cars, hunts for kids and pre-teens will be local and on foot. The geographic range and the degree to which the hunt requires going to others' houses will probably be determined by the participants' age and their street sense.

Which is to say, third-graders can probably tell the difference between coniferous and deciduous trees but won't know their aspen from a holly in the ground. While they will be safe and happy to poke through the grove at the corner, with some parents nearby, they shouldn't be leg-cruising the center of town at nighttime or pounding on stranger's doors at any hour.

Earlier we spoke of scavenger hunts appropriate for either kids or early teens. Let's identify three categories again and add a few more details.

The **Nature Scavenger Hunt** would be perfect for that corner grove. Arm each trooper with a plastic bag and a list of things they should find, like a white rock, a yellow leaf, a seed, a grain of sand, a pine needle, a twig shorter than their thumb, an insect, a piece of litter, a cigarette butt, a pine cone, anything else you see there in sufficient abundance when you check out the grove in advance. They can play this individually or you can put them in groups.

You may even want to "plant" odd items to increase the volume of treasure, like poker chips, pennies, name tags, address labels—anything that others won't walk off with in advance or the resident critters won't consume or hide.

While there, you can note the areas where the hunters shouldn't go, to tell them before they begin—or to mark with little red flags indicating out-of-bounds.

Figure out a time limit, like 20 minutes, and be insistent that nothing can be removed from anything alive; the needles, seeds, cones, and so on must be on the ground to count.

Finally, if they are very young or sheltered, some may not be familiar with the items on the list, so you may need an example of each to show them right before you blow a whistle and send them off!

Another form of the nature hunt, for older kids, teens, and even adults, is the **Alphabetical Nature Game**.

Here they are expected to bring in as many of 26 items as they can find, each starting with a different letter in the alphabet: A might be an ant; B, a birch leaf; C, a curlew or crocodile. Just kidding. Nothing live but insects, if you even want to include them. This is probably best played by groups, who must stay near each other during the hunt.

To toughen it up, you can give them points only if the letters of the items found are successively bunched. For example, they may find items beginning with ABCDE but no F, then GHIJ but no KL, then MNOP but no Q, then RSTUVW but no XY, then Z. The longest successive bunch is six (RSTUVW), so that is their score. By the conventional system, their score would be 20.

The third scavenger hunt might be done inside a house and would best be done by early teens or even adults. Here, each team is given a list of things to get—from each other!

The lists would include items people often wear or keep in their pocket or purse. (Thus I'd mix teams: half male, half female.) Like a key, comb, glasses, pen or pencil, ID card, photo of somebody else, lipstick, brass knuckles, lint, perfume, stick of gum, items of clothing or jewelry, a body hair.... They could even barter an item from another team, swapping something they have in excess for something the other team will give.

This hunt shouldn't take very long, perhaps 10 minutes. It might be a warm-up or a quick game inserted in a lull.

Of course, everything goes back to its original bearer when the game ends, unless the host is short of chewing gum.

Another favorite old party book was Mary Robb's *Making Teen Parties Click* (Stackpole Books, 1965). While the example is 35+ years old, it would still work today. Robb suggests that two teams sit at different ends of the room, in rows equidistant from and facing a common table. The host calls out items one at a time. Say, a brown shoelace. Team members who have such a shoelace extract it from their shoe and, once in hand, race to put it on the table first! (They must have the item in their hand before they can leave their chair.) Once a winner is declared, all put their shoelaces back and await the next item.

The 24 items Robb suggested, other than the shoelace, were an aspirin tablet, pocket comb, white glove, wooden pencil, straight pin, canceled stamp, rubber band, white hankie, stick of gum, lady's belt, white sock, $1 bill, nail file, paper clip, boy's picture, girl's picture, tie clasp, red shoe, man's belt, safety pin, pocket knife, bobby pin, 5-cent stamp. (Alas, your list will need considerable updating for today's teens!)

For years we've had magazine hunt where a list of items were cut out within a set time period.

Today most teens are computer savvy, and if there were enough computers and web lines, an updated variation would put teams to an Internet Hunt. Again, a list is created of things findable by computer. You can request two things: the fact being sought (Lou Boudreau's middle name, where Seneca was born, today's opening stock price of ATT, the name of the University of Chicago stadium under which the early atomic work was done, the northernmost city in Finland...) and the page on which the fact was located (quickly checkable if you suspect the answers are invented). Set the time limit and off they go.

Later we will give a list of the kinds of things one might seek on a scavenger hunt. The format couldn't be simpler: a person or team, a list, a deadline, supervision if needed, and loads of fun in between. Then a noisy to-do as the items are displayed and the prizes are given!

## Scavenger Hunts for Adults

Adult scavenger hunts are closer to the traditional mold, where normally serious, proud souls of legal age (or thereabouts) are foisted on an unsuspecting populace to beg, grovel, cajole, and otherwise wheedle useless heirlooms and edible oddities so they, the beggars, can win a prize!

Why would door answerers let this ragtag horde into their homes and scurry to provide it with a brass baby pin, a cat's tooth, and an okra sprout? Because they're embarrassed? Afraid? Eager to get rid of the cackling menace? Maybe they too are daft.

More likely they get into the spirit because at some earlier time, in a moment of social despair, they too were one of the hapless beggars trading their standing for a newt's egg or 1986 penny. Or because the group is having fun, is harmless, and they want to share the infectious spirit. Anyway, if somebody wants to carry away, forever, a broken broom handle, a banjo pick, and the bones of beloved Fido, so much less for the knackers!

Some scavenger hunts limit themselves to physical things to be secured from homes. I like to add in commercial establishments too, lest they miss all the fun. Little things that generally require no purchase: a matchbook cover from a bar or a paper napkin with the fast food name on it.

I also like to include on the hunt list information that any respondent might be able to provide, like the full name and correct spelling of the current mayor or the middle name of Harry Truman. Sometimes the person visited knows the data, can call a friend, or will look it up in a home reference book.

For variety, you can force the hunters to be particularly selective in the people sought. Once, in Guayaquil, Ecuador, I sent a horde of Peace Corps volunteers and other friends into the city to complete a treasure/scavenger hunt, part of which included a clue written in Chinese. (I had asked a Chinese restaurant owner to first translate the clue for me.) Off went the nefarious bands in search of wandering Chinese. Smarter were those who headed straight for Chinese restaurants because, unknown to me, the translator had a wry sense of humor. Not only did the clue ask the reader to give the people a particular number, the translator added in a plea for them to also give these foreign beggars a bit of food for their audacity!

But there is another kind of scavenger hunt, mentioned for children and early teens in the last chapter, that doesn't require leaving the home at all.

Let me update six classical categories first introduced by Mulac and Marion Holmes about time Ike was President! Many of these can be done by individuals or teams.

The **Pocket Scavenger Hunt**, for example, has the players going into their pockets, purses, or back packs for such items as a letter ready to mail, a handkerchief with a hole in it, a pill, a quarter, a half-stick of gum, a note with a person's name on it, a lottery ticket, or a receipt.

An expansion of this is the **Mother-and-Daughter Scavenger Hunt**, to combine what they are wearing or carrying in their pocketbooks. That might include the items just mentioned, or black socks or stockings, a pin, lip gloss, a photo of a man, a comb minus at least one tooth, a green bow, breath mints, something made by hand by the bearer...

A **Book Scavenger Hunt** is a quick ice breaker. Pile up a dozen books, or lead them to your bookshelf. Let the team pick any one book. Give them a list of pointmakers, have them turn to page 49, and begin scouring to see how they tally up. Make up your own list, something like one point for every capital letter on that page, another every time the word "the" appears, two points for every numeral, two for every adverb ending in "ly," three for every gerund, five for every word in italics, ten every time the word "wonderful" is found—some 10-15 categories in total. Highest number wins.

A tougher contest they call the **Just-around-you Hunt**. Here, teams write on a sheet of paper their responses to items found inside one room, which isn't limited to the furnishings and can include items worn by or of the participants. Compose a list of 10-15 things they must note, like as many items as they can find made of cotton, of wool, and of silk; the different woods (and their names) used in the room; the different ways leather was used; the four-legged objects found, and the different kinds of glass used in the room.

A great warmer is the **Statistical Treasure Hunt**, which can be played anywhere and only requires that teams of equal size gather and tally!

Again, you make up the items and points according to your guests' ages and backgrounds. Some of the point-gainers they suggest are (1) counting January as one point, February as two, and so on, add up the total number of birthday month points on your team; (2) total all the shoe sizes added together—one foot per person!; (3) add 10 points per 1000 (or 100) for the total number of miles traveled by each member to get to the gathering; (4) add the total of all waist measures they will admit to; (5) add the total number of (legitimate) children they have, with sets of twins five points more, grandchildren three more each, and triplets 25 points more; (6) add five more points each for other continents visited; (7) add the total number of pennies teammates have in their pockets or purses times four; (8) add the number of states (or foreign countries) each team member has lived in for longer than five years, and so on, having fun with the list and the adjusting the point totals to reflect the group's values.

# Scavenger Hunt Problems

Some of the same safety, time/space, and matching problems explained for treasure hunts exist for scavenger hunts too.

A major concern is the hours during which your ruffians will be banging on other's doors. Daytime is little problem, although many folks won't be home. After 10 p.m. is probably too late. Before 7 is still suppertime in many homes, so the safest period is probably 7-9:30 or 10 at night.

Selecting the right houses to solicit items should remove most of the big concerns. Well-lit family homes in solid neighborhoods would be my first targets. Crack houses, tenements, and lowlife dives would be my last.

Excessive exuberance probably takes care of itself since it would likely scare away potential door openers.

Violation of solicitation laws might also get you a stern warning from the local gendarmes, though it has never happened at my hunts nor have I ever heard of it occurring.

Spending the rest of the hunt and night in the hoosegow for other reasons is the greatest fear of the host and hunters. Two things can help there: (1) a note indicating that the team is on a treasure/scavenger hunt, and (2) the hunters staying out of places likely to bring police action: on private property, atop buildings, under porches—in short, horsing around where you shouldn't be!

What kind of a note might you give each team? Depending upon the seriousness you want it to convey, it might be some deviation of this:

---

To Whom It May Concern:

The four oafish souls bearing this note are involved in a treasure/scavenger hunt in (city) from 7:30-9:45 p.m. tonight (date). If they are acting up, please scold them roundly. If you need further assistance, please call me at (phone number)!

(Your name)

---

We'll see another variation of this note later.

Finally, anything unlawful is to be avoided, from excessive speeding, drinking and driving, or the 1000 other crimes people can commit. The team staying together helps prevent harmless fun from getting excessive. Usually one or two sober, grounded minds nip anything unlawful in the bud.

# Designing a Framework
# for a Super Party

Now that we know what treasure and scavenger hunts are, how they can be adapted to players of various ages, and a few of the problems that can be linked to them, let's pick out the best elements, exercise the most prudent precautions, and create a dynamite party by combining both!

Let's start with some assumptions: that you want to give a party that will never be forgotten for the very best reasons, because it was so much fun and there was so much activity the invitees can hardly wait to come to next year's repeat!

A party that simply makes it impossible not to participate joyously, draws upon everybody's intelligence and vigor, and calls for both teamwork (which helps those present to get to know their co-partners better and mix more) and individual effort (which helps them know and like themselves more).

And a party that gives prizes to the winners, festive memories to every participant, and abundant food to all!

To do that right you need a general framework for the festivities. A broad schedule and scope into which all of the activities comfortably fit. Which means a setting, starting and ending hour, a guest list, sufficient time to get everybody invited and the party organized, a theme (if desired), invitations composed and sent, prizes bought (and maybe wrapped), food planned and fixed, the hunts designed, clues created and composed, sites checked and "plants" left, and about 117 more details attended to.

Sound overwhelming? Not a bit, as long as you have every detail listed, sorted into some sensible time order, and systematically tended to. It's easier if you have a spouse, friend, or even a relative help out!

Let's look at each element of a Super Party so you can pick from the comments, plus anything else that occurs to you, those items needed for your checklist.

## Broad Schedule and Scope

A broad schedule means to me painting with a barn brush. It suggests a 20-minute gathering period; 10 minutes to pick teams and give a rough explanation of the range and rules; five minutes for the teams to plan strategy before leaving; two hours for the guests to assail your neighbors and the town; 15 minutes to get back safely; another 45 to fortify themselves with food and drink; 30-45 minutes to hear bad poetry and tales of derring-do (some true), see questionable scavenger items (like green chicken feathers and a penny with an Indian head glued on), pick a winning team, and give them prizes; then some dancing or another short game or two; plenty of kibitzing with new and old friends, and everybody out at the sound of the bell. All adjustable, nothing too rigid except the two hours and the 15-minute return time.

If your crowd needs two hours to eat and drink before dividing up the spoils, so be it. If they need appetizers-on-the-spit and flagons of nonalcoholic spirits before the plunder of your fair town, fine. If they are very slow learners and need 20 minutes to hear and absorb the directions, what's the rush? If you want them to dance until the rooster crows in desperation, great! It's your party. You simply need some broad schedule or you'll be giving out prizes before the hunt and saying goodbye before hello.

As for the scope, just how far do you want the hellions to roam without a leash? Two miles in any direction? To the red line on the map that each team gets and no farther? Who cares, the farther the better?

And whom do you want them to harry? Not your next-door neighbor? Lester's police-calling aunt on Bell Avenue? So which streets, if any, are out-of-bounds for scavenging?

That will also be influenced by whether they are hunting on foot or driving, the weather, their sobriety, and how many are over 90.

# Setting

Setting means where they will be sitting. Where the group will compose itself first, repose later, gallantly pose at prize time, and perhaps decompose on the dance floor. In other words, on which rug or floor will these hunters spit, grind their butts, shake their frame, and spill libations? (Yes, I know. Not *my* friends.)

Plan for the worst, then figure where these firebrands will all fit at two times: (1) when the directions are given, and (2) when the scavenger items are shown and the prizes awarded. You can feed them at a distant trough and dance them in the coop—it's the sitting times you must consider. Count the chairs, figure that some will sit on the floor and a few will hunker by the door, and that tells you how many to invite (plus a few more: every party needs enthusiastic no-shows).

It also suggests that the rare Etruscan bric-a-brac on the table and the soap statue of Lady Godiva by the door might be wisely hidden in the attic closet until the last dancer has swirled into the night. The dog and mice will hide themselves.

One last thought: that rug, their shoes, and rain or snow. As a last resort, shoes off at the door when they arrive, perhaps, but when they return for sure. They can put them back on after their soles have dried, to dance. You'll also have to crank the heat up to keep the floor warm.

# Starting Time

According to our broad schedule the party would have to last at least four hours, then perhaps an hour or two more for dancing. Five to six hours: a long time in contemporary America, when dinners over 25 minutes and conversations two paragraphs long make folks antsy.

So when do you start? If it's a Sunday (or Saturday) afternoon gathering, you might begin at 1 or 2 p.m., with supper the post-hunt feast. The logic of a day party is that the driving and hunting are easier and probably safer, and you might get one of your older kids to take the younger ones to the movie or skating, then to McDonalds.

On a Friday or Saturday night, 7 p.m. seems to be the magic hour, with plenty of snacks and light beverage mandatory for those who must rush straight there from work or other demands and are inadequately fueled.

The Super Party may be too long to be held on a weeknight if many of the hunters have worked all day and must return to work early the next morning. And while I prefer Sunday night parties, few others do. They want to go back to church or see "60 Minutes" and a movie, to rest up for a workday.

# Ending Hour

That's partially up to you and partially up to the guests, unless you state an hour, ring a bell, and firmly heave the malingerers out.

The afternoon gatherers will likely depart soon after the food is eaten and the prizes awarded, those with kids heading home, the rest, if bitten by a dancing bug, toward music and stronger potions.

Nighttime departures can be slower. They're there, the music is playing, a spirit of fun lurks, the baby-sitter is asleep, they don't want to break the spell and leave their new friends. Whether you want to bring it to a halt or wait 30 minutes and let the energy subside on its own, well, again, it's your party.

But you can lock up the booze and beer at a certain point after the prizes are out and the dancing begins, particularly if you have told them earlier that because you're concerned about their getting home sober and safe that's what you plan to do. Fix more coffee, keep the pop and punch flowing, and play the music until the last howler drops. Then try to see that nobody drives who shouldn't:

sofas and blankets available for all who would rather stay for breakfast.

## Guest List

Who do you invite? Who do you "overlook"? And who is intentionally left out?

If it's an adult party, you intentionally leave out the kids. Period. But who's a kid? If it's no kids no way, post-high school is the minimum—or 25 or 40, you determine. If you want to be a bit more lenient, particularly at an afternoon hunt, you can lower it to high school: if they're in it or older, they're invited. Younger than that, they simply aren't mature enough.

The exception is the afternoon family party where every family is a team. Then they can decide if they want to bring and endure Baby Betty or Bub, carsick and cranky.

Who do you invite? Anybody you would enjoy having there and who would fit in with the rest. Everyone will be expected to participate so if it's clear that they can't or won't, you invite them knowing that you will have to entertain them while the others are gone and you're also trying to fix food, get the oil spot off the floor, and find a missing prize. If they'll pitch in, all the better.

Don't exclude them because you don't think they're clever enough to figure out codes or complex clues. Every team can carry a person whose gifts are elsewhere. They're just as likely to be the scavenger hunt whiz who will get the pink cupcake and know that pistons are parts of cars and not toilets.

Centuries ago I spent a weekend in a small rural town called Inhambupe in northeastern Brazil. Electricity was a new addition, from the line linking Paulo Afonso Falls to Salvador. It came on punctually at 6 p.m. and went off promptly at 10. A man in town had that job: he turned the electricity on and off.

So if you had a party in Inhambupe, you invited that man. And if he had a good enough time to be detained, or if the spirits were of a sufficient vintage that time assumed a new dimension, the lights stayed on and everybody knew that your party had been a smashing success!

Thus, if your town is like Inhambupe and it's important that others know that your hunt is a winner, invite the electricity man. Or sole constable. Or biggest gossip.

I'd overlook the group drunk who, at any starting hour, will appear all sails to the wind and insistent that he not only can navigate, he *will!* Sadly, that means his spouse as well.

I'd overlook jerks, losers, violent types who will punch out teammates who come up with different clue solutions, the loony, just-split couples where vendettas have been uttered, and anybody who simply can't tolerate someone else you'd rather have there.

Remember, it's your party. Better a super time had by all, including you, than having to fret all night about a likely misfit.

How do you explain their exclusion to them later? You don't, unless they bring it up. Then you tell them you didn't think they'd have fun because _____. Fill that in with a thing or two they dislike, whether or not there was much of it at the party (like too much noise, too little, too much crazy driving, thunder, too many academics, too many jerks). They'll be glad you were so considerate.

## Time to Invite Guests and Organize the Party

What kind of lead time do you need to get your party together, prepare invitations, get them out, tally the responses, contact the silent minority, and do it all up right?

A key factor is whether this will be a theme party. (More on this in the next section.) If that theme is date- or season-based, you have a range of dates within which your party must be held.

If you want it to be a Halloween party, it should probably be that night or, more likely, on the weekend before (or even after, though that's stretching it.)

If it's a Valentine's Day Couples party, same thing: a week before or after is about as far as you can go. But a "Winterfest" can last from cold to warm, though early is always better than late. Better December than late February.

Theme parties, particularly those with set dates, create other difficulties. It can be a date when families expect to celebrate together, like Christmas Day. Or it can be a long weekend when travel takes place, like the Thursday to Sunday of Thanksgiving. Both will cut heavily into your attendance unless you can artfully schedule around the occasion.

As for time, it shouldn't take any longer than two weeks to put the Super Party together, and faster the second or third time. Just divide the detailed checklist into day-by-day activities for those 14 days and meet the mini-deadlines.

I'd send the invitations out a month in advance, if possible. Then check the nonrespondents by phone after two weeks, to make sure the invitation arrived and to get an idea as to whether they might attend. Some legitimately won't know until almost that day; others gain attention by delaying their response.

Between us, at a Super Party it really doesn't matter if you have last-minute additions as long as you know that a solid core will take part. But all hunters must be at the party by the starting time to be included in the team formation. Let them know that no teams will be formed or sent out once the hunt has begun. (Some may want to form their own team and will come late for just that reason. Those teams scare me most: too little of the sobering influence a mixed team brings to keep the driving in bounds and the shenanigans to a minimum.)

How many hunters do you need to have a party? You need at least three per team, better with four. At least two teams, much better with many more. So 6-60. Most parties probably have 12-20 on the hunt.

# A Theme

Theme parties directly affect scheduling, as we mentioned. Themes can also affect attire, décor, music, food, other games played after the hunt, and prizes. This is particularly the case for kids' parties, even for early teens, as we saw in the earlier examples in this book.

A St. Patrick's Day Party is a case in point. Nobody is admitted without a gaudy display of green, with a prize given for the best male and female Irish attire. Green hats and green shoes are particularly encouraged.

You could hang green crepe about and shamrocks in key areas, prepare tags adding "Mc_____" or "O'_____" before their names,  and use green tablecloths, paper plates, and napkins at the settings.

An Irish tape or CD in the background might play lilting songs from Erin, while all could be taught a simple jig later to start the dancing. The punch could be green, as might as much of the food as possible without making it looking moldy or nauseous. You might slip in another game, made Irish by a change in the rules or terminology. Finally, the prizes could fit the theme. Small boxes of "The Olde Sod" might be a loving remembrance to all who join the hunt. (Olde is right. It's been in your garden almost forever.)

Theme attire is particularly popular. It lets the partakers do something special in preparation for the gathering, then gives them a chance to display their craft or cleverness in an approved way. By having all dressed differently for a special purpose and around a common theme, it creates a unique bonding for that night. (Cynics would say that they all look like fools together.)

Just make sure that their attire won't impede their driving or movement during the hunt. Nobody wants a dandy looking but dead or maimed leprechaun a lingering party distaste.

## Composing and Sending Invitations

What kind of invitations do you send?

They have to contain the five w's and h: who, what, why, where, when, and how. Something like

> "Terrie and Tim Thomas invite you to attend a Super Party at their house (1234 Fifth Street, Happytown) from 7 p.m. until midnight, Friday, June 17. Please R.S.V.P. by mail or call 345-6789."

You can elaborate upon that many ways: expand upon the kind of party and upon what they must or might wish to do to take part. You can also make the invitation part of the treasure hunt theme. Its message might be invisible or in code. (More on how that's done when we talk about creating and composing clues.)

## Buying (and Wrapping) Prizes

You have to give the winning team members something. It can be unforgettable—an actual, shining new BMW sports-something apiece or a group, expense-paid excursion to Bali. (Don't forget to invite your favorite how-to treasure/scavenger hunt book author to that party!) Or it can be somewhat more modest, like a yard of fog or a hug from each of your drooling children.

Even a lot smaller, suggests Margaret Mulac, who advocates awarding TV's, refrigerators, stoves, or automobiles—in the toy size. All the better if the first one given is wrapped in the appropriate, huge box, inside of which is a wee box containing the true prize!

Whatever it is it should be in keeping with the amount of effort the people expend. Better if it's something they can take home and either use regularly or see repeatedly. And nice, if you have a theme party, if it's in keeping with the theme.

If you had the St. Patrick's Day party we discussed, maybe a $10 food/beverage ticket per winner to use at Clancy Muldoon's Wild Irish Hot House. Too steep for your budget? Why not a bottle of some Irish ale for each victor? (Don't worry, the teetotalers will give it away as a prize to somebody else!) To carry the treasure hunt concept to its fullest, those could easily be buried (unwrapped) in a small chest at a final site.

Neutral gifts are the best because you never know how the teams will be sexually composed. Certificates give the greatest freedom to the winners, trophies are fun (but expensive), and unisex scarves and thermal one-size-fits-all socks work.

I like to continue the suspense right into the prize-giving. Have the winners sit on the sofa, put four boxes of equal size on the mantel, and get out a deck of cards. Each draws, ace high, jokers low. The holder of the highest card gets first choice of the boxes, the second, second choice, ... The problem, as you've told them, is that one box contains $20 worth of steaks. Two boxes have gifts worth about $10 each. And one box, if you remember correctly, is filled with sawdust.

Alas, for those with a sense of humor truly tainted, two of the boxes might have a bit of steak juice inconspicuously dribbled on a corner, barely visible from the sofa. (One does contain the steak.) And one has the slightest fleck of sawdust clinging to another corner. (No, it doesn't contain the sawdust.)

Another way to add more fun to the hunt is to throw in additional prizes. They could be won several ways.

One, at certain clue sites, where the teams are seeking numbers, you could also scatter something readily visible: poker chips, playing cards, business cards, something they can't just go to the store and buy by the dozen! Each is worth a prize.

Or certain scavenger items, or a certain combination of items, might be worth a prize. One such item might be the *haiku* or the poem the team composes. The best of those might be worth one prize, with the team selecting the person to get it. (That could be done by drawing playing cards too: high person wins.)

The best costume, male and female, deserves a prize. And the biggest stick-in-the-mud, usually awarded unanimously, might win a booby prize (a candy bar, for sweetening, is inoffensive). You stretch the list.

As for wrapping the prizes, fine if it's part of the fun (as with the steaks and sawdust), adds to the theme (covering them in diapers on New Year's Day), or you think it adds class to the gathering. But giving gifts unwrapped is acceptable too: it's cheaper, faster, and lets everybody see the gift at the same time.

How they are wrapped can add to the fun. A certificate or a paper cutout in a TV box, for example. But do that to just one item. The joke is thin the second time, and a drag thereafter.

Or the box, in keeping with a treasure hunt motif, may contain only a clue as to what should be inside. That might be a riddle with three possible answers. Whichever they guess they get. Second place is second guess, and third, third.

## Planning and Fixing Food

You don't want me even suggesting specific edibles, an aging bachelor whose idea of *haute cuisine* leads to a slit-top microwave special, with a salad chaser and a glass of milk.

Still, you have to feed the salivating horde you sent scurrying countywide for more than two hours. And fast or they'll start toothing on your doilies and chair arms.

Match the food to the theme, if any, and the setting, which is probably more Boy Scout or Boot Camp in sophistication than grand opera. *Crepe de* anything, flaming entrées, and finger bowls are for a different kind of gathering. Consider Sloppy Joes, burgers, burritos, hot dogs, hobo stew, chili, spaghetti, salad (probably green or potato), ears of sweet corn, garlic bread, chips—all in abundance!—plus some alternatives for the vegetarians or truly dieting.

Prepare what you can in advance. The rest is a matter of getting it warm (on a cold day or night they'll want it hot) just as they return, taking their wraps, and pointing them at it.

Nothing wrong either with having several buckets of hot chicken wings, an assortment of giant pizzas (does anybody anywhere eat anchovies?), or a burroload of tacos delivered.

Back it up with easy-to-pour beverages, ice evident and in abundance, and plenty of coffee and hot water for tea. If there's a bar for alcoholic drinks, also stock some nonalcoholic beer and perhaps some spirited but spiritless punch. If it's a BYOB party, leave out labels and a pen so bringers can identify their bottle. Start it off by putting a label "FOR ANYBODY" on a couple of house bottles you are contributing.

## Time to Plan the Hunt!

Let's focus next on designing the hunt itself, which requires a chapter of its own. Then another chapter about creating and composing clues, and checking the site and leaving "plants" a short time before the horde arrives and is released back on society. And finally, the final touches of the Super Party.

# Combining the Hunts

Now that we've designed a flexible framework, we need to focus on the hunt itself.

Rather, hunts. Let's combine the best of both kinds, treasure and scavenger, to keep every participant fully involved for 120 breathless minutes.

At the hunts in which I participated I saw three glaring weaknesses.

One, the four people in the car spent about five minutes solving the clues, then held on white-knuckled for 115 minutes zooming from place to place. The driver was stressed. The rest of us held our breath and each other, jumped out when the car screeched to a stop, found the item (or didn't), jumped back in, and raced off again. The emphasis was on car speed and cornering skill, too often driven by the very person with whom, in other circumstances, we would never have soberly ridden!

Two, there was almost no thinking power involved.

Three, the hunt was one-dimensional. We had two choices. The first was to find the clues, usually in a set order; the second, not to find them but to park instead at a beer hall, tope and tell jokes, and return to the guest house two hours later.

Why not plan a Super Party around the most challenging hunt possible?

That means tough clues for the treasure hunt locations.

Alternate ways to earn points: scavenger items, some found in nature; some obtained from people; others, available at places en route.

Plus bonus brainstormers that hunters can create while going from here to there—or at that beer hall, a fast food hideaway, or even in your front room!

The idea is to have too many things to do so they must collectively select the best ways to use their time and accumulate points. To have activities by which all of the members of the group can stay simultaneously busy and involved: one drives, another solves clues, a third figures out where they can gather acorns or sidewalk cracks near a clue site, while a fourth writes a poem or tries to unscramble a point-earning anacrostic.

Let's discuss each of these elements in the chapters that follow.

One piece of business yet to do here. Determine how to award points, or at least pose the idea now that by how we reward various accomplishments we can direct the actions, and to a lesser degree the safety, of the hunt.

If you give 15 points for every treasure hunt number correctly found, 3 points for each scavenger hunt item, and 1/2 point for every brainteaser, it'll be a pedal-to-the-metal night, with brains on vacation.

If it's reversed, why bother to leave your house? Play the brain games, and if any time is left hit your neighbors for a squash or yearbook picture.

The way things are done will also be influenced by the difficulty in finding the scavenger hunt items and the length of that list. You could give 50 points for Archimedes' will or a unicorn hair and who would bother? (And if they did, are you sure you want them at your party?) On the other hand, a point per grain of sand will have any sane group finding shovels and heading to the beach.

What might influence how the points can be earned?

The weather and driving conditions. On a lousy night you can give the farthest clues far less value than those nearby, and clues in general less than brainwork or scavenger items in the city park a block away.

How much do you want your wards tromping in the forest or neighbors' lawns? If you don't, delete all clues or scavenger items that require it—or devalue them mightily.

Their age. Conversely, older players—well out of their teens—might drive perfectly well and delight at cruising from spot to spot but don't get as enthused about prancing door-to-door or ferreting for toadstools in the wilderness. Design and reward appropriately!

So we combine the two hunts into one and devise a point system that rewards wit and creativity as well as hustle. But first we need challenging treasure hunt clues, a spirited scavenger hunt list, and some worthy brainstormers. Read on!

# Creating and Composing
# Treasure Hunt Clues

We want the treasure hunt clues to be challenging but not indecipherable or impossible.

As mentioned earlier, I far prefer the proliferation system where teams seek numbers at the destination sites and receive all of their clues at the beginning, to solve in the order they choose—or reject as they wish.

Yet, since they see all of the clues at once, it is probably best to mix fairly easy, straightforward clues with others that are more complex or challenging. That way they won't reject the hunt out of hand. They can also pursue the simpler clue while others in the car are solving some or all of the rest.

Clues can be created and composed in many ways: as prose or.poetry, in riddles or puzzles, by scrambling the words, to require some act or performance, without text whatsoever (it's there but invisible), in code, on a map, written in another tongue, as a drawing.... Let's explore these possibilities.

## Prose

An uncomplicated, straightforward clue in prose will surely confuse the team. It looks too simple. There must be some trick.

*Add the evening ticket cost for an adult to the earliest viewing hour on Saturday to the number of upstairs urinals and you have the magic number of "A Perfect World."*

If that movie is showing only at the Bijou, it first shows at noon (12) on Saturday, there are nine urinals in the men's room upstairs, and regular patrons pay $6 at that hour, the answer is 27. It is simple, no tricks.

One or two of those will get the team started while they try to unfold the more complicated clues.

## Poetry

Use poetry whenever possible. It looks very hard but is in fact easy to write—at least bad poetry.
For example, let's use the clue above and simply switch it into poetic form:

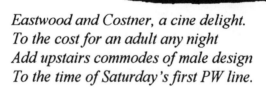

*Eastwood and Costner, a cine delight.*
*To the cost for an adult any night*
*Add upstairs commodes of male design*
*To the time of Saturday's first PW line.*

No poetry prize here, but it is fairly straightforward. Eastwood and Costner are movie stars and "cine" means cinema, so all that's missing is the Bijou. The rest paints it out: add the cost of an adult ticket to the number of upstairs urinals to the earliest Saturday starting hour of "PW," of the movie starring Eastwood and Costner, "A Perfect World." Once they look in the newspaper and see what movie features both men, they'll get the title and know to go to the Bijou.

As for the process of creating bad poetry, here's how I do it. This is expert advice. I've written more bad poetry than I can poke with a pentameter.

Start with the essentials. Write down what the hunter must know from the poem:

movie title (or key actors)
where it's playing (can look that up or call)
the adult fare at night
number of upstairs urinals (in the two-story building)
starting matinee hour of that movie

The word "night" caught me first as an easy rhymer, so I wrote out that line: "the cost for an adult any night." Then I wrote down "Eastwood and Costner" because I knew that Clint stars with Kevin in the movie, and that way I can get them thinking theater, movie, and title so they will go to the Bijou. (To make it a bit harder I could have said "Clint and Kevin.")

I need more words that end in "..ight" to finish that rhyming line so I run the alphabet using letters before "..ight" to see if any make sense in this context:

| blight | indict | plight |
|--------|--------|--------|
| delight | light | relight |
| fright | might | slight |

None rings a bell. But if I plug in a short word or two in front, to match the length and flow of the other line, some possibilities suggest themselves:

"a movie delight"
"a cine delight"
"a copper's delight"
"a cop's delight"
"a kid's fright"
"a kidnapper's delight"

You can surely think of more. The last four assume some knowledge of the movie that even if known would only reconfirm what a newspaper tells: "A Perfect World" is the flick. I want to indicate the place it is being shown so the team would know to go there. So the second worked best.

What have we got so far?

*Eastwood and Costner, a cine delight*
*The cost for an adult any night*

That order seems best so I can get them thinking theater first, then what to do when they get there. Okay for starters. I also want to match the number of meters or feet in the rhyming lines, if possible. Counting the accented words gives me the number and rhythm: both lines are a rough four feet long.

Now I must work on the last two lines, then I can adjust, if needed. It's always needed.

"Urinals" is hard to rhyme with so I'll put it toward the front of one line. I want to include "upstairs" (or "top-floor") with "urinal." I'll try "Upstairs urinals..."

In the remaining line I have to get them to discover the starting time of the earliest showing of "A Perfect World." (Why? Because I've been to the Bijou and know the first weekend movie starts at an even hour, 12. But if it began at

11:35 and the last show began at 9, I'd be looking for the last showing—and the clue number would be 24. Adjust the variables to create good clues and acceptable poetry. Just so it's a calculable number, who cares what it is, other than the team searching for it?)

I want "the time of Saturday's first 'A Perfect World' showing." Since they must know the movie title to find the right theater, I could shorten that to "PW." What happens at that hour? Eager patrons form a line. So I could have them find "the time of Saturday's first PW line."

Let's put that down, then see if I can finish that remaining line to rhyme with it:

> *upstairs urinals*
> *the time of Saturday's first PW line*

What rhymes with "line" and makes sense when referring to urinals?

| | | |
|---|---|---|
| brine | pine | vine |
| dine | Rhine | wine |
| fine | sign | design |
| mine | stein | resign |
| nine | tine | malign |

Dine or wine? Just missed. The word "design" rings best, and of course since urinals are designed for males that could work. Let's plug it into the first two lines and see what we have.

> *Eastwood and Costner, a cine delight*
> *The cost for an adult, any night*
> *upstairs urinals of male design*
> *the time of Saturday's first PW line*

I could slip in another word for "urinals" and make it a pinch harder. Perhaps "latrines," "cans," or "commodes," which in the male form would suggest urinals.

Looks confusing and hard but it isn't if you know in advance what you want and what they must pluck from the clue.

More important, what's missing is what I want them to do with all of these facts: add them together. Except for the first line, so I'll put a period there. To the cost I want them to add the number of urinals, then add the starting hour. So I adjust the lines and throw in a final period:

> *Eastwood and Costner, a cine delight.*
> *To the cost for an adult any night*
> *Add upstairs commodes of male design*
> *And the time of Saturday's first PW line.*

Put as many clues in poetic form as possible and the hunters will be amazed at your brilliance, sensitivity, and artistic legerdemain. Just don't try to pass as a poet in other circles!

## More Poetry, by Format

Another way is to put the clue into a format poem, as suggested in Robert V. Master's *The Family Game Book* (Doubleday, 1967). First select a 4-letter word. (Or a 5- or 6-letter word; the longer it is, the longer your poem must be.) This word, solved, gets them to the clue site. If not, you must expand the clue farther or alter it internally.

Let's say our word is "pool." The city has one pool so by guessing that word the hunters should be off, swimmingly. The poem starts each line this way:

"The first is in _____,
The second is in _____,
The third is in _____,
The fourth is in _____."

After each line write a word that begins with the respective letter: "P" in the first, "0" the second, "0" the third, and "L" the fourth. Then make sure the last word in each extended line does not include that letter.

So it might read like this:

*"The first is in pass, but not in Wasser.*
*The second is in oar, but not in water.*
*The third is in orc, but not in mate.*
*The last is in look ... by the gate. "*

I warned you about bad poetry. AABB, the last words in the first two lines rhyme, as do the last words in the last two. When using this format I always try to slip in more information in the latter half of the line or in the rhyming words chosen. For example, at the expense of a slight meter break in the fourth line, I can insert the key location clue, since the gate is where the number is. Using the word "pass" in the first line lets me ease in another clue: a pool pass is the way to heaven on a sweltering summer day. Even the words Wasser, oar, water, orc, and mate have water connotations.

Let me say it again: these seem impossible to write for those who never dabbled with poetry. Malarkey. Find a set of words to put before the commas that have the same number of feet (one syllable, two, three...). Then see if you can switch them for other words the same feet lengths that are more suggestive of the clue site.

For example, I first chose "pink," "oats," "oaf," and "lake." Then I set my mind thinking of water- or pool-related words that began with the same letters and were one syllable long. "Oar" came to mind but I had to skim the dictionary to find "orc." (To most it means a whale but it also can be any other cetacean defined by early writers as a "sea monster." Our pool was short of these.)

While I was at it, I figured what I needed for the ending. Since the clue was at the "gate," that had to be one of the endings. Once again I mentally sounded the alphabet with an "ate" ending to see what came up. Like bait, crate, date, fate, hate, late, mate... (I picked "mate" over "bait" because one doesn't fish in our city pool!)

"Water" was a natural ending word, but it's hard to rhyme with. Except with itself: "*Wasser*" is water in German, and pronounced almost the same. Two for the price of one! So they went with the first two lines, since neither contains a "p" or "o."

Next came the refining and actually matching.

"Pink" had nothing to do with a pool so I needed another word starting with "p" one syllable long. "Pass" popped into mind. Bingo: the key words for line one were "pass" and "*Wasser.*" Then "oar" and "water" worked for line two. "Orc" was okay for three, with "mate," since I needed to end the last line with "gate." The first word for the fourth line, "lake," was misleading, since the city also has a lake. So I needed another word starting with an "l." I wrote it all out, putting "l_____" in that spot. It became obvious that by dropping the comma and inserting an ellipsis

(...) I could instruct them to "look" by the gate, which is precisely what I wanted them to do!

Writing this kind of a clue is just a lot of word play, making lists, checking the dictionary (there are actually rhyming dictionaries in the library!), "running" the alphabet, and seeing what words work best in each spot. Hardly a reader of this book couldn't improve on my final clue above, but it worked so I used it (though I hoped "oar" and "orc" didn't send them to the lake, which is orcless—I hope!—but not oarless).

# Riddles

You know riddles. "What's _____? Your mother-in-law!"

Except here the answer is what they must seek, after resolving the riddle you pose.

Let's suppose you have a train station in town, it's open to the public until midnight, the train schedules are posted on a wallboard behind a glass cover, and the train from Brighton arrives at 3:17 p.m. You want the team to bring back that number.

So you might pose this riddle:

> *It's scheduled on tires of steel,*
> *stops in town knowing its station,*
> *and links a rhyme with "right on!"*
> *When does it deliver "right on" fare?*

By playing with the key words you could even pound that into some loose poetic form, though it looks less like a riddle:

*Scheduled on tires of steel, there*
*it stops, knowing its station.*
*Linked with a rhyme for "right on!"*
*When does it leave that human fare?*

Whether it's a riddle or a poetic clue is really unimportant. What counts is that the team has to scramble mentally to figure it out, then ends up physically at the right place seeking the right thing. As important, fun was had in the process.

## Word Squares

One kind of puzzle you might use as a clue reads the same vertically and horizontally. Hints are given so the person knows which three words are needed to compose it.

Let's assume that in your town there is a Bob's Cab Company, and that, logically, it has a telephone number! That's all we need for the clue.

The form the team will receive will look like this:

|   | 1 | 2 | 3 |
|---|---|---|---|
| 1 |   |   |   |
| 2 |   |   |   |
| 3 |   |   |   |

To solve this clue it must be filled in this way:

|   | 1 | 2 | 3 |
|---|---|---|---|
| 1 | C | A | B |
| 2 | A | N | O |
| 3 | B | O | B |

The answer is the phone number (ANO) to Bob's (BOB) Cab Company (CAB).

What hints might we offer that will get them to provide the right three words? These might do:

(1) Shared by a train engine, taxi, and the Civil Aeronautics Board. (For your information, but not included in the clues: The first has a cab, the second is one, and the initials of the third are C.A.B.)

(2) What you want to bring back; we owe it to Bell (ANO=a number). (But unless we add in "we owe it to Bell" or some brighter hint of a telephone, they might chase the cabs around town trying to catch their license number,

stop or call for their operating license number, or God knows what else.)

(3) Apple dip, pendant, shilling, or a docked tail. (All are "bob's.")

Use the dictionary to make certain your clues are correct.

Word Squares aren't easy to do if more than three letters are required, and extremely hard beyond four, so if you can't tell all in three or four words or you can't definitively fine-tune the message in the hints, it's probably better to spend your time creating other kinds of clues. But dabble a bit and try. You'd be surprised how often you can find the precise, wee words that will get your hunters on track.

## A Mixed Message

The clues must vary in difficulty or the hunters will never leave your den or driveway. Mixed messages are fairly simple.

One way to write them is to mix up the letters in each word of the clue. Unmixed, they are headed to the spot!

In its simplest form, this might be the clue with the letters in the right order:

GO TO THE SOUTHWEST CORNER
OF THE JOHNSON MORTUARY.
RATHER THAN DEATH
THIS NUMBER SPEAKS OF BIRTH.

But how might the team members first see this clue that will lead them to the date the mortuary was established, as noted on their large sign on the southwest corner?

OG OT EHT WSESUHTOT NERROC
OF HET NSONHOJ UAMROTYR.
TRRAEH ANHT ATDHE
SIHT RMBUNE SSAEKP OF HTIBR.

Alas, that might be too simple. You know your guests better than I. If you want to mix it up a bit more, why not switch the order of the words around in each row? Something like:

UAMROTYR WSESUHT~OT OG NERROC
OF TO HET NSONHOJEHT.
TRRAEH HTIBR ATDHE
SIHT RMBUNE ANHT OF SSAEKP.

There are ways to make it even harder. Much harder. But this is hard enough or you'll have hunters hunting for you!

## The Collective Fool Clue

One of my favorites forces the team to test its true mettle before the world. Rather than creeping through parks and up ravines in the dark, this clue obliges them to beg loudly, in unison, in a very public place. My favorites are fast food restaurants.

Usually I have spoken with the shift manager and explained what is up: several groups of four will come in independently and form a line near the counter, then recite some doggerel in unison. They are part of a treasure hunt, and their treasure is a number. All they want is that number, though they'll probably buy food anyway. Would she or he indulge these demented souls, and when they finish this free entertainment simply give them the number "12345"?

I assure the person that the whole thing will take about 10 seconds at most per group, provide a lot of fun for the customers and crew, and will surely win the store lifetime devotees because of her/his good will. Appeal to their good nature. I've never been turned down.

This stunt is always a lot of fun for all involved. But you can squeeze even more fun out of it. When you give the opening instructions for the hunt, mention that one of the clues is a dead-end. So if you go to or do what you are told and no number is evident or given, hurry on to the next clue.

Of course the dead-end clue is the one where the team must cavort the loudest, to the drop-jawed horror of the salesfolk and customers. Nobody knows what's happening, and when they ask for a number, even more confusion reigns. Since the venture is harmless enough and the team will leave quickly, the police are never involved. Retelling this activity gets the heartiest laughs at the postmortem party!

Alas, why should one fast food outlet have all the fun? When this is a dead-end clue, I put down a different store or address on each set of clues.

What precisely must the group, and the clue, say? You can compose any ditty that doesn't take much time. An example might look like this:

> *Burger King, near the Bank of America on Broadway, is eagerly awaiting the arrival of the "Hunt Chanters"—you, collectively, holding hands in a line parallel to the counter and saying loudly and together.*
>
> *"Oh greet manager! The Grand Swami sent us to get a MAGIC NUMBER!" (Then bow. If done in unison, the manager will indeed give you the number!)*

Sometimes.

## Invisibility

Why not simply have an empty page containing one of the clues? Not totally empty: it might say, Clue ___ on it.

Alas, nothing is as it appears in a Treasure Hunt. The words are there, as a scrambled poem, so even if they find them the task isn't too easy.

The simplest way to make invisible clues is to use lemon juice and a bit of water, then write the message with a stylus. There's also something called Adam's ink that you can buy at party stores. To see both you must warm the paper up. Putting it near a lamp or lighter will do. Just remember to find a clue writer with legible writing!

## In Code

Team members usually expect one or several coded clues if your hunt is at all advanced. Don't let them down. You just can't use a code designed to fool CIA cryptographers.

The simplest is probably the best: numbers for letters, letters for numbers, and all punctuation or like symbols written in. In other words:

| | | |
|---|---|---|
| 1 = A | 13 = M | 25 = Y |
| 2 = B | 14 = N | 26 = Z |
| 3 = C | 15 = O | A = 1 |
| 4 = D | 16 = P | B = 2 |
| 5 = E | 17 = Q | C = 3 |
| 6 = F | 18 = R | D = 4 |
| 7 = G | 19 = S | E = 5 |
| 8 = H | 20 = T | F = 6 |
| 9 = I | 21 = U | G = 7 |
| 10 = J | 22 = V | H = 8 |
| 11 = K | 23 = W | I = 9 |
| 12 = L | 24 = X | J = 10 ... |

Then you write out the message, using blank lines to show where they are to fill in the correct letters or words. Below each blank line you put the corresponding code number or letter. That is, every time an "E" is needed you write "5." So even if they never catch on to the extraordinarily clever system we have devised, should they guess that 20-8-5 is "THE," they could then fill in every T, H, and E and might be able to continue deciphering the clue by further logic, magic, guesswork, and innate genius.

This is how an example might look:

____ (23) ____ (8) ____ (1) ____ (20) / ____ (11) ____
(9) ____ (14) ____ (4) / ____ (15) ____ (6) / ____ (2)
____ (1) ____ (12) ____ (12) / ____ (9) ____ (19) / ____
(20) ____ (23) ____ (15) / ____ (20) ____ (9) ____ (13)
____ (5) ____ (19) / ____ (6) ____ (15) ____ (21) ____
(18) ? ____ (16) ____ (12) ____ (21) ____ (14) ____ (7)
____ (5) ____ (4) / ____ (2) ____ (21) ____ (20) / ____
(13) ____ (9) ____ (12) ____ (12) ____ (5) ____ (18) ____
(5) ____ (4) , / ____ (13) ____ (1) ____ (18) ____ (11)
____ (5) ____ (4) / ____ (15) ____ (22) ____ (5) ____
(18) / ____ (20) ____ (8) ____ (5) / ____ (4) ____ (15)
____ (15) ____ (18) .

Which, when decoded, reads:

*What kind of ball*
*Is squared 1 time more?*
*Plunged but millered,*
*Marked over the door.*

A ball that is two times four is an eight ball, which brings to mind pool. On Miller Avenue, say, is the "8 Ball Pool Hall." The local pool is known in slang as "the plunge," thus what is plunged is a pool. And the number we want is above the door, or the address.

Even without determining the code a puzzle guesser would figure out much of the clue. The question mark indicates that the first word would probably start with a "w" or "h" (who, what, why, where, when, or how start most questions), which then would suggest that a "W" is number 23. The letter "A" as a code among all number clues (which stand for letters) probably means that "A" stands for a number. And a long guess, since it is the first letter, might suggest that A = 1, the first letter. Which further suggests that, in reverse, 1 = A. Tentatively putting an "A" for every "1" looks promising, since the first word, starting a question, then becomes "W _ A _ ," which is likely "what." And that means 8 = H and 20 = T.

Filling in the spaces for 8 and 20, the second to last word then becomes "T H _ ," which is surely "the," and that means E = 5. Again filing in every 5 with an "E," they fall in the right spots, since many words in English end with "E" or find it in the penultimate position before a "D" or an "S."

Another clue is the eleventh word, "_ _ T." That is likely "but" or "yet." With the "E" not filling that center spot and "B" and "U" still not decoded, let's make 2 = B and 21 = U, and fill in the rest of those that way.

Two more words now reveal themselves. The fourth word, B A _ _, with the last two letters the same, could only be BALL, BARR, or BASS. So 12 = L, R, or S.

And the third from the last word, A B _ _ E , preceding the word "the," is likely ABOVE. Is "0" the fifteenth letter in the alphabet? Is "V" the twenty-second? So 12 = L, the earlier word is BALL, and after we fill in those three letters it's just a matter of counting out the rest of the letters, completing the clue, and zipping down Miller Street to the pool hall to get the address—or, if you want to take the gamble, looking in the phone book!

If you want to make the decoding tougher, but not impossible, you can work in reverse (Z=1, A=26), skip a few numbers but keep them in order (C=1, Z=24, A=25, B=26), put the vowels first, then the consonants (A=1, E=2, B=6), or reverse that. Just be sure that the clue itself, once decoded, is easy enough to understand and find or you will have very angry hunters later on!

If you're new to codes and puzzles and you think this coded clue is too difficult either to compose or solve, pick up an edition of the *Dell Crosswords and Variety Puzzles*. Check both the "Anacrostics" and the "Figgerits." Both are somewhat easier than the clue above since they provide definitions that lead to the letters. Create a clue built on either design.

# A Map

Shades of "Ye olde-fashioned treasure hunt"! But why not? Even better if there's a bit of pacing or measuring, finding a tree with a mossy hump, some hard ENE reckoning, and a shovel casually leaning next to some freshly turned soil.

Decades back I was invited to the most elaborate hunt I'd ever heard of given annually by a group of Christian Scientists in the suburbs of Chicago. One of the clues involved a map that led us to a coffin. A team member had to open the lid, get in, close it, and endure creepy sounds to extract a number played by a hidden recorder.

Another led us to a tire pump at the edge of a lake. We pumped with vigor to inflate a dummy that rose from the middle of the water bearing a number on its chest!

The point? The map has to lead somewhere exciting. An adventure not too dangerous but worth the taking.

A simple map clue might look like this:

| | | | Shannon Street | |
|---|---|---|---|---|
| ZLC | P | | | |
| | L | X | Start in center of lot | |
| | | | and go 40 yds E / | |
| | | | 35 yds ESE / | J |
| | | | 10 yds N / Look E | a |
| | | | | n |
| | | Eric Street | | St |

Which means that team members will park in the Zion Lutheran Church lot and start walking at about the middle of that lot, park side, go 40 yards due east, 35 yards ESE, 10 yards north, and look east.

What will they find? A 35 m.p.h. sign starting them straight in the eye. Or a park bench with a number somewhere on it. Or a 10-yard marker on the field. Or a scoreboard on which you've posted 100 for the home team, O for the visitors. That's the number they need.

It's more fun if there's a surprise at the end. If the map leads the team to a tree with a hollow root. Naturally they will look all around the root, then reach in—to find nothing! But if they just looked upward the number is tied firmly to the branches many yards above! (You must take it down the next day!)

Or if in the hollow you had left another map (in fact, one for every team) that took them further afield. Or gave them explicit instructions, or a riddle, poem, puzzle, or anything else irksome that impeded immediate gratification! The problem is that somebody may remove those items from the hollow. So this is best done in remote areas and with the agreement from all teams that, in the spirit of teamwork and fun, should there be a direction note at any site, they promise not to remove the companion notes for the other teams!

## In a Foreign Language

What is more vexing than a clue in a foreign tongue that nobody on the team speaks or reads?

How do they solve it? They could find somebody who does, get a cross-language dictionary and pull it apart word-by-word, take wild guesses, or chuck it.

A simple clue might read like this:

*Ixrupa mexclaptix pie odzlimcu faxorndi lemon.*

*La suma de todos los naipes diamantes que tienen números.*

*Du brauchst die Summe aller Karo Spielkarten mit Nummern.*

*Hai bisogno della somma di tutte le carte di quadri con i numeri.*

That's actually three times easier than most other clues once you've deciphered a tongue. Not only does it say precisely what you need—the sum of all the diamond playing cards with numbers, or 54—but it says so in three languages. The fourth—why not put it first to bedevil those of good faith?—is not a known language, though it does like lemon pie.

If you include Spanish, as I've done here, some of the message can usually be guessed. And some of your team members may speak it, or at it. They can call their grandmother or the team can head to the local taqueria or bodega.

It's fun to include Chinese, copy the written form, and paste that into the clue when you make your copies at the local Quick Print. That will spirit the group off to some Chinese friend or establishment—or they will interrogate some bewildered Korean passerby.

Just be sure to double-check the clue for accuracy. It's too tempting for a person put upon to translate your silly clue to say instead, "This team begs to be tied up and eaten for breakfast."

Some lingering thoughts. If many of your guests do speak another tongue and you write clues in it, be sure that each team has at least one member who can read that language. And make the clues as hard as they would be in English.

Or take that language and doctor it up. Create Pig German or Pig Polish just like we make Pig Latin. Have fun with it so the team members do too.

## As a Drawing

This needn't be creative art. It can be a paste-up of ads or slogans or anything that, put together, gets the team to a spot that yields a magic number:

All you do is cut out what you need, usually from a newspaper or magazine; draw by hand what is missing; adhere (probably with rubber cement or glue stick) what you want the team to see in some order, and make copies of it to include that night.

There is no end to clues that can be created this way. Let me describe two.

One you've seen 50 times, particularly when you were a kid, so it should be easy to envision. It's a drawing that is full of errors, usually with a line asking, "What's wrong here?" Things like a cat reading the newspaper, water flowing uphill, people wearing two different shoes or with them pointed backward rather than forward, third eyes, a picture on the wall warning "Hem Sweat Hem," plus things less subtle. You draw or copy such a picture. The team's task is to count the number of errors in it.

The second is based on something you find in print. Let's imagine there is an advertisement in a current, major magazine selling bicycle tires that glow in the dark, purchasable only by mail. So you paste up selected parts of that ad and magazine. On the bottom of the master copy you tell the hunters the number they are seeking: the cost of one set of 700 x 28C (C-83) tires, with shipping but no tax.

What you include in the clue is part of the ad itself (excluding, of course, the printed price of those tires plus shipping), the masthead of the magazine (with the editor's name, address, and pertinent info except the actual magazine title), perhaps the order form (with the specific numbers they need deleted), the magazine's barcode, and perhaps a key identifying item from the magazine's cover, such as the Seal on the magazine I previously mentioned, *Dell Crosswords and Variety Puzzles*, that identifies it as "No. 1 in Puzzles."

The easiest way for the team to solve this clue is to go to the magazine rack, get the right edition, and thumb through until they find the ad and the magic number(s). (Be certain that the magazine is sold at local stores open at the time of the hunt!)

Alas, how will they know it came from that magazine?

The seal or key item from the cover will help them find it on the rack. The bar code tells which magazine, if they can charm the checkout soul to scan it for them at the front counter. They at least know how much it costs, since that is usually listed somewhere near the barcode for magazines. The editor's name might help, and could be used in the library with the current *Writer's Market, Literary Market Place,* or similar guide to locate the magazine.

If that's not enough, they could guess!

# Twenty-first Century Tools

A great treasure/scavenger hunt hardly needs new-fangled tools at all, beyond paper, pencil, some sturdy shoe leather, and a watch.

But why not use what's available that will enhance the fun even more?

If you find this book in the attic and your folks, or theirs, used it to delight and baffle their friends, you will laugh at what I think is contemporary and wonder why I didn't include the high-speed, carbon-lined zilchmo or the faster-than-sound revaporizer. For the same reason that my folks never talked about the Internet or the digital camera. They didn't exist—and my folks, like me, were too timid to walk around in daylight and discuss unknown things with even less known words.

But it is the twenty-first century and two items should be integrated into the second, updated version. (If you can think of more, use them too. But you still need clues...)

# The Internet

The Internet, of course, presumes the existence and use of the computer, itself an anathema to those still uncertain about the future of inside plumbing.

By having players or teams collectively beam up to the Internet, they are no longer limited to the boundaries of the map nor to things that must be seen, touched, and brought back. If they can decipher the clues, this expands their possibilities immensely.

For one thing, the "party" could in fact be, to you, a two- or many-phased thing.

You could invite your guests to two parties: the first, two hours alone at their own computer solving clues by finding the indicated items, answers to be emailed to you at the closing bell. The clues would be posted at your or a friendly website and accessible only at the starting moment, with the directions and related instructions posted 15 minutes earlier.

The second "party," that night or soon after, would be to get these atomized invitees together, to discuss the Internet hunt, eat, drink, and have fun. Or to go on a second-half scavenger hunt, this time hunting as teams, with the prizes to be a combination score of both hunts. Then the party! (If you want to see the many ways computers can be used in "treasure hunts," simply post those words at yahoo.com or, better, google.com, and check out the list of sites that pop up.)

It would be much harder to use computers, one per team or person, at your home or the party site, unless it was something like a computer lab and it had Internet access for all of the players simultaneously. Or if each brought individually linked laptops... Yet this eliminates half the fun by removing the collective bustle. Four around a computer? Give me a No-Doze.

Having said that, there's no reason why several items sought in the Scavenger Hunt couldn't be accessible by computer only. Since by the hunt's rules you can't go to your own house (or use your own laptop if it happens to be in your car or purse), that would create the two-tiered challenge of first getting somebody to let you quickly use their machine, then actually being able to extract the needed data or printout fast enough to warrant pursuing that object.

## Digital Cameras

While these are bit expensive as I write this update and few are likely to have one in their glove compartment, if at all, when they become sufficiently commonplace to have such a camera available for each team, what a way to get visual proof on a disk that you in fact found the respective sites!

Even better for Scavenger Hunts, there would be no need to bag fer-de-lances or pluck purple leaves from trees. All the nature objects could be captured digitally, then shown to the assembled, breathless crowd on a monitor later, along with the "extra" shot of Susie being held at bay by a watchdog while her teammates try to decide whether to distract the salivating canine or run for their own lives!

Pictures of specific types of people, of people in specific situations, of a clock at a particular time...clever minds will find 50 uses for a digital camera in a treasure or scavenger hunt.

Just be certain that the batteries are charged and will last for the number of shots required!

# Developing a Scavenger Hunt List

Once you've decided to have a combination party, guess which lucky person gets to develop the scavenger hunt list?

How else can you keep the others, if they're invited, from squirreling away the oddities before the big night? ("You won't believe what I happened to find in a bag in the woods...!")

The only question is how hard the items must be to find, how many items you want to list, where you want your parolees to go, and how much loot you think your neighbors and the community will let them beg or purloin.

What goes on a scavenger hunt list?

From nature, some things easily found and in season, some that are around but not common or particularly evident, and other things that take a bit of daring or cunning to secure. But nothing that does any real damage to the ecology, hurts critters or your hunters, or has much monetary worth.

From people or places, it's about the same. Mostly odd, hard-to-find, low value items that border on being junk or useless memorabilia. Things you needn't return. I like to include knowledge bits that people might know and contribute, even if they can't provide the extra turnip with a missing bite or a doughnut with three holes.

How do you create ingenious scavenger hunt lists? Don't. If they are too clever, the teams will ignore them. Just list things you see in nature, or might; or things that people—especially odd people—might have around the house; or peculiar, quirky things that somebody just might know.

Once you have them written down, leave some as they are and define others more fully. Not an ice cube. Anybody can get an ice cube. But one that is at least 1" long when turned in. That requires thought and planning.

Not a red ribbon. A red ribbon with traces of yellow in it—exactly 7" long! Then they must find a red ribbon and cut it to 7," exactly. If it already has yellow in it, winner. But a bit of yellow paint streaked on, or a blond hair woven in, or even a page of legal paper taped to it, winner again. Big traces but traces nonetheless. Make it a game. Fun on all sides. Not running but running on one leg blowing kisses!

Start with the list below and pluck out what might work. I'd limit my party list to about 25-30 items total, as much from nature as your locale, safety, and the weather suggest and your invitees would enjoy. The rest to be begged from the unsuspecting populace or local stores. They can be listed separately, as they are below, or mixed so the team must segregate them at hunt time.

There's nothing special about the list that follows. If something on it would work for you, use it. If it prompts a better idea, all the better!

# From Nature

pine cone between 3/4" and 1" long
plum
2 smooth white stones
3 hairs from a horse's tail
3 acorns
maple leaf
6" of red gossamer
snowflake
two ounces of Bermuda grass clippings
leaf with three colors in it
exact latitude, longitude, and altitude of host's town
dead leaf the same length as the driver's shoe or hand
blade of grass exactly 4" long
5 three-leaf clovers
clump of crab grass
worm 1" or longer
corn tassel

# From People or Places

pressed and dried natural flower
matchbook from a local bar
gray hair
celluloid collar
gym shoe with red stripe
toothpick in cellophane wrapping
15 grains of popped pop corn
airplane boarding pass
cop's autograph, with badge number
names of the smallest and largest mammals

used pipe cleaner
package of pumpkin seeds
belt buckle, without the belt
a newspaper column in Spanish
funniest thing you can find
small American flag (under 8" in length)
ice cube more than 1" long when delivered
doughnut with three holes
pencil with electric blue lead
chicken feather (without chicken)
8" mop of hair
calories per serving of Franco-American chicken gravy
1991 copy of *Time Magazine* with man on cover
3 needles threaded with blue thread
horseshoe
sock with hole worn in it
an artificial daisy
turnip with bite out of it
full name of the town mayor, spelled correctly
date Bolivar met San Martín in Guayaquil
beard hair over 3" long, with name of donor
true name of Sholom Aleichem
pompon feather
oil for a red lamp
7 3/16" of virgin shoreline
empty can of cream soda
name and home phone number of current high school
    homecoming queen
dimensions of the letter "C" in the City Hall sign
popsicle stick
postcard that accompanied a free product in the mail
lint ball
name of one fighter who lost in championship bout to
    Joe Louis, with site and year of loss

auto registration slip
6" of unused waxed dental floss
chlorinated pool water
glass marble
1" plastic pipe 1/2" in diameter
elephant imitation
raw peanut
today's closing of the most expensive stock on the NASDAQ market
first name of the inventor of the Waring blender
last sung word of Puccini's *La Boheme*
first five words of any Dolly Parsons song
confetti
ATM receipt
picture of a person in a helmet
Portuguese phrase asking your grandmother for her blessing
straw in paper wrapping
torn movie ticket or stub
hand print from infant
6" square of calico cloth
home town of Ted Williams or Kenny Rogers
instrument string
first name of one team member written or impressed on a French fry
credit card application form
travel brochure about France, Italy, or Bulgaria
name of owner of Chicago Cubs when present scoreboard was installed in Wrigley Field
yellow hand hair
full lip print on banana skin
"Have a Happy Day!" sign
in Windows 98, steps you must take to put an em dash in your text

twopenny nail
leprechaun
church key
business card from a real estate broker
packet of crackers in plastic wrapper, intact
strand of cooked spaghetti
ad for R-rated movie
discount coupon for soap
Roy Rogers' real name
bookmark with a website printed on it
ball point pen that writes in four colors
Chinese symbol for "Happy New Year," plus name of
    the animal of the current Chinese year
name of medication to cure the crabs
small mustard packet, half-empty
name of manager at local 7-11 (give address of store),
    plus height in centimeters
hours when local library closes on Tuesdays
one stained tooth in an envelope
five-pronged fork
pinch of paprika
middle name of Harry Truman
Oriental potpourri
capital of Tibet
footprint of a high-heeled shoe
raw fettuccini noodle
the dedication in Michener's *Centennial*, transcribed by
    four people
name of baseball pitcher with the most single-season
    wins
toilet brush hair
medical term for flat feet
piece of coal
can of elbow grease

# Adding Bonus Brainstormers

There's some creativity required to solve the clues and find the treasure hunt sites, and a morsel of it needed to collect scavenger items, but too little to really challenge team members whose strength is cerebral rather than athletic and tricky.

So why not inject a third element that involves all of the team members, some to a greater degree, and adds an additional challenge? Something that can be done at your house before the team departs, in the car or elsewhere during the hunt, and again back at your place before the "turn-in" hour strikes.

I call these "brainstormers." Some, the team members create. Some come from things they dredge from memory, to commit to paper. And some have a scavenger hunt element to them: they may require finding something, then adapting it to the specific hunt format.

Whatever the requirement, these add another layer of action by which the team members can gain more points. They also require the group to prioritize their activities, then call upon the individual members to contribute their knowledge and skills beyond simply driving or riding in a car and leaping out at each clue site.

So here are some starter suggestions. Add to this list. Make it fit your players' abilities and fun threshold. If most of them are colleagues from the math department, include math games, puzzles, or activities. If they are computer whizzes, find something similarly appropriate and insert a byte or two to satisfy their appetites.

# Brainstormers

12-line iambic poem that mentions five items to be handed in from this scavenger list

written sidewalk interview: "the most embarrassing thing ever said" to three people (with their names, ages, vocations)

a written one-liner

"*Et tu, Brute!*" written in conventional Pig Latin

note (less than 18 words long) that praises the _____ (host, local team, Chicago Cubs) that includes every letter in the alphabet

plot of "Elephant Man" in exactly 20 words

nickname that reads the same frontward and backward

list with the correctly spelled name of every person in attendance at this party

hand-drawn diagram of the inside of the team's car: include 15 marked details

short written joke that mentions both spats and a mermaid; must be funny!

*haiku* mentioning a tree

two-verse song with original lyrics, to be performed by group later at party

alphabetized list of stores or commercial establishments in _____ (town or city); ___ point(s) for every consecutive 6-letter (ABCDEF) block (without repeating any letters)

itemized list of the number of original teeth of all the members of your team

synchronized cheer given by all team members at party, in praise of Abraham Lincoln and the emancipation; must last at least 15 seconds and include the word "YES!"

# A "Magic Checklist"

It's with the greatest apprehension that this "Magic Checklist" is even suggested. Inevitably I will forget some minor detail—like "fix supper"—and you will toss this poor text into oblivion. (I birthed this humble booklet: be kind to it. If you must, toss me.)

Please use the checklist in the sense in which it is offered. It is a rough organizational guide based mainly on ideas developed in the earlier chapters, plus a few more items not worthy of prose before.

It's your party. If you want to start six months earlier than suggested, go to it. If you want to start thinking about what the group might eat after you've sent them off on the hunt, more power to you. (I trust your cupboard isn't bare!) Fill in more details, move whole sections around, cross out what doesn't fit, underline and circle what you think you'll surely forget....

But do one thing first: take this book down to the Quick Copy shop, make a copy or two of the checklist to decorate in any color you wish, and leave the original as is. Why? Because fun hunts are like those potato chips advertised on TV, it's hard to give just one. You'll want the unsoiled checklist to copy again. And again.

The "magic?" It's like building a ski chalet or an eight-layer cake. All those instructions, all that hope, so much work, so many details, and wham, in a flash, it's all together and even better than originally envisioned! Like all magic, it works if you work.

A few of the items could use greater elaboration. I've noted an (*) after those. Let me discuss them further in the chapter that follows.

# The "Magic Checklist"

<u>One to several months before the actual party:</u>

\_\_\_\_\_ select a tentative date

\_\_\_\_\_ select a theme, if desired

\_\_\_\_\_ decide whether you want to offer a treasure hunt, scavenger hunt, brainstormers, a mix, all three, or something altogether different

\_\_\_\_\_ select a location for the party and the specific rooms you will use

\_\_\_\_\_ if the party is to be held elsewhere, begin necessary arrangements to secure that location

\_\_\_\_\_ tentatively pick a starting time for the gathering

\_\_\_\_\_ consider whether you will have a fixed final hour, and, if so, what hour

\_\_\_\_\_ plan a rough itinerary of the party

\_\_\_\_\_ prepare a desired guest list

\_\_\_\_\_ check tentative date, hours, and itinerary with specific key invitees (*)

<u>About a month before the actual party:</u>

\_\_\_\_\_ if the party is to be held elsewhere, begin necessary arrangements to secure the location

\_\_\_\_\_ prepare invitations, with a map included to the party site

_____ mail invitations (optional: including small, self-addressed, stamped envelope for reply)

Within about two weeks of the party:

_____ call the invitees who have not responded
_____ invite more people if responses are lower than you wish
_____ finalize the party structure and itinerary
_____ determine what you will give prizes for and the number needed
_____ buy the prizes
_____ wrap the prizes, if necessary
_____ prepare treasure hunt clues, a scavenger hunt list, and brainstormers
_____ get CD or recorder player (plus speakers, if needed) if you plan to have music playing at the party
_____ find theme music to play, if desired
_____ make arrangements for the care of your children (or other dependents or residents) if they are to be out of the house during the party
_____ prepare team hunt packets (*)
_____ prepare name tags
_____ buy theme decoration items, if desired
_____ plan food and beverages for the party, including special theme-related edibles
_____ buy needed nonperishable food and beverages

The day before or same day as the party:

_____ borrow additional chairs, tables, plates, etc., if needed
_____ buy perishable food

_____ prepare as much food in advance as possible, to be heated or finalized that day/evening before being served

_____ double-check all sites to be sure all numbers are present

_____ leave "plants," if any

_____ make certain your house and address are visible; perhaps locate easily seen signs at key corners for newcomers, even a large sign on your front door

_____ thoroughly clean the house, particularly the rooms to be used

_____ provide extra washroom supplies, such as toilet tissue and paper; leave where they are easily visible

Before first guests arrive:

_____ hide anything valuable that might be damaged or stolen

_____ lock doors to all rooms you don't want entered

_____ turn on music to play quietly in the background (*)

_____ if it's wet or snowy outside, provide a shoe mat by door

_____ prepare a table or easily accessible bed where coats can be kept for the short time before the hunt (*)

When the guests arrive:

_____ one of the hosts should greet each guest at the door

_____ the other host should help the guests out of their coats, mix, find the light snack and nonalcoholic drink table, seating, and the washroom(s)

_____ gather the guests together to explain how the hunt works (*)

_____ help in the picking of teams (*)

_____ perhaps distribute gas money to the drivers (*)
_____ help the new teams gather together for a five-minute
      planning session
_____ send the teams out to hunt

While the guests are hunting:

_____ if desired or necessary, have one host out overseeing
      the teams' external activities and the hunt route
_____ spot cleanup of the earlier gathering site
_____ final food preparation
_____ quick check of the washrooms

As the teams return:

_____ greet each team as it returns
_____ remind the members how much time they have re-
      maining before all clues are due and help them find a
      place to gather to work on the brainstormers until
      final moment
_____ collect all clues at the appointed hour
_____ direct the guests to the food and beverages
_____ after eating, gather the group together to announce
      the preliminary team totals (*)
_____ announce what remains before a winner is chosen:
      team "performances" (*)
_____ let each team perform (*)
_____ have the other guests vote (*)
_____ announce the winning team, with appropriate bows
_____ give prizes to winning team members
_____ give other prizes
_____ put out snack food and beverages for the rest of the
      evening; can switch to nonalcoholic beverages, if de-
      sired

_____ start more games, if any

_____ start the music for dancing

_____ have a separate, quieter area for chatting

_____ send partygoers home

_____ provide sleeping cot(s) and blankets for those who shouldn't be driving or who prefer to sleep before leaving

_____ collapse!

# Finally, a Super Party!

What we've done so far is describe the many parts of a fun party, hopefully the best party you've ever given and the best your friends will have ever attended!

All that remains to do is put the elements together so everything takes place when and where it should, the folks enjoy themselves, nobody gets hurt, and the guests can't wait for their next invitation!

The previous chapter provided a "magic checklist" built around a rough organizational schedule that should help co-ordinate your actions and remind you of what is to be done when.

A few of the items on that checklist, though, could use further explanation, so let's do that in this chapter, before ending with an encouraging pat where you like to receive encouraging pats to propel you into action!

## Key Guests

Most people when planning a party have a certain cadre of close friends they really want to entertain, plus others they'd like to add to the mix. Said differently, if certain friends can't or won't attend, they'd rather not give the party at all.

That being the case, draw up your plans, select the best date and hours for you, develop a rough itinerary and explanation of what would transpire at the party, and test it against those core friends. Tell them precisely what you're doing: making sure they could attend and would enjoy that kind of a gathering before firmly setting the party in motion by arranging a facility, sending out invitations, planning food, and composing the clues.

If the date simply won't work for your friends, you may wish to adjust it until you find one that will. The hours may have to be altered: evening rather than afternoon, start a bit earlier, whatever. Make certain they know that it won't be for children, if that's true. And subtly imply—or flat-out state—that you'll be expecting them. At least ask them to circle that date on their calendar!

And if they are less than frantically enthusiastic about cavorting on a treasure or scavenger hunt, ask why. If their objections can be easily rectified without altering the fun, promise to do so. But if they're just indecisive, tell them this will be a party they'll never forget and that they'll kick themselves for their remaining days if they don't take part. Then make it just that!

If nobody wants to go on a hunt? Throw the whole lot overboard, get some better friends, and be glad you found out so soon!

## Team Packets

Each team should have the same hunt materials, which means that you make one set of everything, head to the

Quick Copy shop, and reproduce the masters as many additional times as needed, plus three: one, in case folks show up at your door who didn't respond to your invitation but came anyway (requiring you to create another team), one for you to have handy by the phone should somebody call with a related question ("a puma chewed our clues and we can't read the first line of #4..."), and the third to go into a file (with the corresponding clue sites penciled in) to be used in the future when you lay out subsequent hunts.

Let's call each team's materials a "packet." What would go in each packet?

(1) treasure hunt clues, probably on a couple of sheets of paper, one side only. (If you want the teams to go to different places in a different order, make clue #1 clue #3 on the second set, clue #5 on the third, etc. Simply write the clue once, without a number, and copy it several times. Then paste the clues in the different order. Give them the pasted version or make a copy. If you give them all the same clues in the same order, teams tend to go to them in that order. As mentioned earlier, some will simply follow the faster thinkers from site to site.)

(2) scavenger hunt list

(3) brainstormers

(4) two or three small (5" x 8") legal pads of paper

(5) four cheap ball-point pens (or as many as there are members of the team)

(6) a map of the area within which treasure hunt sites are located

(7) perhaps a flashlight, if needed. (You might ask which drivers don't have flashlights that work in their car, then provide them with a flashlight.)

(8) a funny note that attests to the fact the group is indeed on a treasure/scavenger hunt, with your name and phone should the person reading the note wish to verify. Why a funny note? So the person reading it, should that be required, will perhaps get into the spirit of the event and will overlook whatever transgression has forced the team to produce the note in the first place. The note might read something like this:

---

To Whom It May Concern:

Yes, this ragamuffin horde is presently taking part in a combination treasure and scavenger hunt. We have asked them to be courteous, brave, and legal— and not to trample flowers or feelings. If you can help them, fine. At least show them compassion: they don't eat if they don't try!

Any questions? Call _____ at _____.

Thanks,

---

Add anything else that is needed to complete the packet. Put it all inside a large manila envelope or a file folder with the sides taped. Then give each team an additional large bag or cardboard box into which they can put the scavenger items.

When you store these items in preparation for the party, leave each team's packet in the bag or box and you'll be ready for the instruction part of the party!

# Background Music

The point here is to turn on the music to play quietly in the background.

I needn't tell you how to turn on the music. The key word is "quietly"! Too much cross-noise makes it hard to greet people and get them to converse with each other at the beginning, makes it difficult to be heard giving instructions, and may even provide some with an excuse or reason to stay (to hear the music) rather than go with their weird team members. So keep it low and very much in the background.

More of the same after the party for similar reasons, until it's time to dance later. In fact, I'd probably leave it off altogether when they return, to let them share the fun and stories that come from the hunt without having to shout over the sound. After the teams have performed and the prizes have been given out, then crank it up as high as you want. Higher when they dance!

# Temporary Coat Holder

Presuming that the guests need a wrap or jacket when they arrive, or later for the hunt, you need a spot close to the front door for them to leave that overgarment during the short time they will be at your place before they begin the quest. That way you can minimize their tracking through the house, at least at the outset.

Three suggestions: (1) temporarily set up a long table with folding legs somewhere near the entrance hall but out of the flow of traffic, (2) use the dining room table, (3) pile them up on a chair in the living room.

How do you explain this oddity? Simply say, "You're going to be needing this coat again soon so let's put it here for now..." It's your party. They'll pretty much do what you say, as long as the wrap is off the floor and lies flat.

If anybody wears a pelt of electric mole or an Inverness cape, they are hardly expecting what your party has in store, and any complaints about their topper being commingled with the more pedestrian slickers and slip-ons will be but the first of many.

After the hunt you may want to store outer garments on the closest bed. Nothing wrong with covering that bed with an additional sheet or even a blanket or two, to keep it clean, particularly if it's wet or snowy outside.

## Explaining How the Hunt Works

Nothing is more important than setting the hunt up right. Most of that comes from the clues, lists, and brainstormers, of course. But the initial explanation is critical too.

You want to collectively greet and welcome your guests, tell them of the exciting venture before them, how teams will be formed, that there are unforgettable prizes (perhaps even what they are) and what the teams must do to get them, the geographic and time limits of the hunt, a few words about courtesy, more words about safety, and what will happen at the party later: food and drink, "presentations," prizes, then open time to unwind, dance, and howl.

After your explanation, you'll help them pick teams, give each team its packet, let teams group together to plan their attack, and at a set time (probably five minutes later) release them to their fates.

THAT MUST BE CLUE NUMBER FOUR!

Do you need a script for the hunt explanation? Rather, let me tell you the heart of what I might say. If some it that works for you, pluck what you need, add and improvise, oversee, then dispatch! (The minute they escape, grab a schnapps and rest a moment. They'll be back!)

"Come on in the living room, everybody, so we can get the hunt on the way!" (Wait until everybody is gathered.)

"We're real happy you could join us tonight. I know many of you had to drive a long way, others had to switch plans around, and most of you had to dragoon your kids to baby-sit or even hire somebody else ... in short, I appreciate your being here.

"Hopefully, the combined treasure and scavenger hunt we've planned will make all that worthwhile. You might even win a fabulous prize! One thing is certain: you'll work up a good appetite for the feast that follows!

"Here's the plan. In just a minute we're going to divide into teams. Each team will earn as many points as it can in the two hours it's on the hunt. The team with the most points wins!

"Each team will receive its own team packet in a few minutes. All of the packets are exactly the same. They will include 10 treasure hunt clues and a map showing the area within which the clue sites are found. What you are seeking at those sites is a specific number, which you'll write next to the clue and turn in later. Incidentally, at a site or two you may have to do something as a group to get that number!

"You'll also receive a scavenger hunt list of things you can get from any place but this house or your own. Some items are also found in nature.

"There's also a third way you can earn points. That will be explained on a list called 'brainstormers,' which will give you something to do while you're driving about in the car!

"You can use only one car and all of the team members must remain within sight or voice of each other at all times. We must rely on you to adhere to that. But not totally. I'll be out on the route too, and if I see any team member completely separated from the others that team will lose 10 points!

"Why would you want to do all this? Because of the stupendous prizes awaiting the top team! You can see them on the table in the dining room. Also, because if you don't play, you don't eat!

"As you'll see by the map all of the treasure hunt sites are within five miles of this house. If you know this area, that means they are between _____ and _____ Streets and _____ and _____ Avenues. You needn't go beyond that either for scavenger items, so those will be the bounds.

"After we pick teams, you'll have a five-minute strategy time here inside the house to figure out where you will go in what order, and who will do which of the brainstormers. You see, not all clues or scavenger items are worth the same number of points, so it does require planning. After the five minutes, all teams will leave at the same time. You have two hours on the hunt, plus a bumper of 15 minutes during which you must return. You can work on the brainstormers here when you're back. The whole thing will end at exactly _____. Anybody returning late loses 10 points a minute!

"A bit about courtesy. You're going to have a lot of fun, count on it. But others are more deprived. They're captive to their TV's or just bopping along, completely unaware of what you're up to. So please, please be courteous and considerate. Stay off flower beds, don't steal, keep the noise to a dull roar...

"Should anybody stop you or not believe that you're on a treasure/scavenger hunt, there will be a note in your packet identifying your mission. But it won't get you out of speeding tickets, parking tickets, or chaos with other citizens!

"I really am concerned about your safety. You're all our friends and it would put a pall on the party later if anything happens to anyone. Don't kid yourself, we will eat anyway—but please be careful. This isn't a speed race driving, which is why I put all the clues nearby. Please stay off the booze if you're the driver—or just let somebody else drive. Other than that, stay together, protect each other, and nothing should happen at all. I also added that 15-minute time period at the end so you'll head back at the end of two hours and be here comfortably before the penalty hour arrives!

"After you return, we'll eat! There'll be lots of food and beverages. Then we'll have some 'presentations,' as part of the brainstormers; I'll tally the points, and we'll give prizes. Then plenty of time to kick back, talk, schmooze, or dance!

"Any questions? (Answer them.) Great. Now let's pick teams!"

# Picking the Teams

Devise a team-picking strategy. You'll undoubtedly have to improvise at the last minute.

First, every team needs a driver. Let's say you expect 24 guests to take part in the hunt and, for starters, they are all heterosexual couples, or 12 per sex. You need six drivers if you have four per team. I'd pick the drivers myself and build teams around them.

I probably know enough about my guests to know which are drunks, which are half-toked half the time, if any have a string of traffic violation long enough to catch an eel, or if any are just plain fools. None on them would be my preferred drivers—or drivers at all!

I'd choose the drivers and call the chosen well before the party. I'd ask them if they would mind driving that night, and tell them I'm asking because I want to keep the hunt as safe as possible and I have a lot of confidence in them that they'd be careful and wouldn't drink before the hunt that evening. If they agreed to that honest flattery (and expectation), great. Most of them would probably be from your core of best friends anyway, so the request would be easy to make.

That leaves 18 unassigned: 12 women, 6 men. I want to have two guys and two gals on each team, and no mates or dates on the same team. So I'd make out three pieces of paper with each driver's name on them, put two per driver in the women's hat and one for each driver in the men's hat.

I'd pass the hat so that each woman could draw out a name. If they drew out their husband/date's name, they'd put it back in the hat and draw again. Finally, I'd let the men who are not drivers draw from a hat to pick a team. Again, if their wife/date was in the same car, they'd have to draw again.

One way to quickly see who is in which car is to have the driver line up in front and as a person joins that team, they get behind the driver.

An alternative way is to have each driver pick team members, in turn. The problem here is the same problem every sandlot kid knows: the last chosen become resentful.

Sometimes some of your six selected drivers aren't too familiar with the area. In that case you can arbitrarily pick one of the other men, who is familiar, for that team. You simply leave that driver's name out of the men's hat, announce your choice, have that person stand behind the driver, and move on. How dare the rest challenge you?

What if the sexes aren't matched? Four too many women over men? Why not make one of the women a driver and book them as the all-lady team? You'll usually know this in advance and can ask a woman to drive beforehand.

Do the best you can. The night won't be a flop if one or two teams have a 3:1 ratio.

The last consideration is the inadvertent matching of two people who truly and wisely detest each other. If you know this in advance, it's often easy to say to another person, "I'd like to balance these teams better. Would you two mind if I switched you, you to this team and you to this one?" One of the people will be elated, of course, and it probably doesn't matter a whit to the other. If they refuse, though, try another combination.

A final step. I suggest you say, "These look like great teams. But maybe some of you want to swap, just so we maintain the same male-to-female ratio and we keep mates and dates apart. If so, let me know in the next minute or so." I don't think anybody has ever switched. But they had a chance!

# Gas Money

It would be a nice touch to give each of the team drivers a bit of gas money. Like $5. Which would probably have to come from you.

It wouldn't be a nice touch to ask each guest to pay $1 apiece to give to the driver. Or to ask them simply to settle up with the driver, though if you did they likely would.

Purely optional.

# Preliminary Team Totals

After the teams return you'll want to collect their treasure hunt numbers, scavenger hunt items, and any brainstormers to be handed in, and tally them up.

Many hunts will have "performance" elements—a poem to be read, song to sing, skit to give—for which they will also be given points.

It's your choice as to whether you want to announce preliminary team totals before the "performances." Team members are eager to know how they stack up against the others, of course, but if you think the wide range of points that will inevitably separate some teams will make those teams out of the running give up and not perform, then it would be wise to wait until the final tally is taken.

Your hunt, your friends, your decision.

This might be an opportunity, however, before the performances" to go through the hunt clues and tell exactly where each site was and the number being sought. Also, where the scavenger item required specific knowledge—like the last word of *La Boheme* or Harry Truman's middle name—here's a chance to share that knowledge.

# Team "Performances"

All that separates one team from the priceless winner's trophies are the points still to be garnered from their team "performances."

So if you include some of the items from the brain-stormers list that require party action when the team returns, now is the time to get the teams to recluster, sit, and either watch the other teams perform or become the stars themselves!

Just make certain that if they must do something together as a group—recite, sing, dance, put on a skit—there is room for that activity, and that the others can comfortably see them while it takes place.

You be the master of ceremonies. Introduce the task at hand and the group, and keep the whole thing fun and moving along briskly. Play with the teams, swooning if appropriate, chiding their genius, suggesting that talent and creativity were unevenly distributed, "fanning" a bad joke or a puny pun, waving signs that match their makeshift offerings, like "help!", "talent need apply!" "this team drinks!" and so on.

The whole idea here is to have fun and give them a way to show off their talents (or lack thereof). So care must be taken to have fun without criticizing or offending anyone. It's to better lampoon broadly, if at all, so it falls on everybody more or less evenly.

## Voting on the "Performances"

There are two ways to go here.

One, the voting is a token thing. If the teams had to write a joke that mentioned spats and a mermaid, and the stipulation was that the joke must be funny, you let them tell their joke, then ask, "Did anybody find that funny?" The rest of that team will likely wave their hands like star-grabbers and probably grunt in unison, which is probably closer to what the joke deserved. But you declare it funny, and they get the points.

The purpose here is to let them show their wit and give the audience a laugh. The voting is a formality. You may want to bypass it altogether, simply announcing that you're about to hear some funny jokes. If the team composed one and somebody on that team will deliver or read it, the team gets the points.

The second way is to make one or several items more competitive. In the brainstormer write-up it might say that the best joke or poem or skit, whatever, earns 10 points, second, five, and the third, three, for example. The write-up would also include all of the stipulations of that activity.

Then at the "presentations" segment each person would be given a voting sheet. If five teams read a poem that they composed, for example, all the guests will be able to vote for the best, second-, and third-best poem read. Even though team members might consistently find their own of-ferings best, so will members of the other teams similarly pick theirs, so that should balance out. You score the voting sheets later, giving 3 for first place, 2 for second, and 1 for third. From those totals come the team totals for the grand prize.

# Awarding the Prizes

When the presentations are over and the final tallies are in, it's prize time!

Make this a lot of fun too.

If you have wee and useless items for the last-place team, wrap them as fancy as possible and play it to the hilt, before they open their bunion sander or patch of remnant cloth.

I mentioned prizes earlier, but one thing is mandatory: lead up to the grand prizes (giving lesser prizes first in rising importance), then have the winning team stand, introduce each person so they can get a hand, make a thing of them actually receiving their prize, then collectively opening them. Snapshots taken regularly, particularly at prize time, adds additional luster.

The showmanship element is important. While the prizes aren't, in fact, a Mercedes or a trip abroad, their awarding is the most important event of the night and the terminating act of hours of attention and pursuit. So to create the proper balance for the night, they must be the highlight.

Of course, a hand to every one of the hunters from all of the teams is then in order!

Once you've reached this apex of group activity, it then makes sense for the group to let its hair down for the rest of the evening, rehash the hunt to the degree new friends want to, move on to other activities, dance, and generally bask in the fun of a contest well entered and valiantly fought.

# A Dynamite Party!

I'm not sure I like that word "dynamite," but you get the idea. Enjoy yourself from the day you decide to give the party until the last howler somersaults out the door.

Enjoy yourself? You who must do all the work, write the clues, heat the food, and weave a thousand strands into a brilliant new cloth?

You bet! Bask in the creation of a party better than any you've attended, a party that your friends will recall long after you've joined the "party animal's eternal." Who else but you was clever enough to bring all the pieces together and unfurl that joyously unforgettable afternoon or evening of fun?

This book is a primer and a prod. You are the creator and the party chief. Now get to it! Become a party immortal!

# Index

Also available from
# COMMUNICATION UNLIMITED

| BURGETT BOOKS | |
|---|---|
| *Title* | *Price* |

| | |
|---|---|
| How to Create Your Own Super Second Life: | |
| What Are You Going to Do With Your Extra 30 Years? | $ 19.95 |
| Travel Writer's Guide | 14.95 |
| Publishing to Niche Markets | 14.95 |
| Empire-Building by Writing and Speaking | 12.95 |
| Niche Marketing for Writers, Speakers, and Entrepreneurs | 14.95 |
| Treasure and Scavenger Hunts | 17.95 |

| BURGETT SEMINAR AUDIO CASSETTE SERIES | |
|---|---|
| (with full workbooks) | |
| How to Set Up and Market Your Own Seminar (3 hrs) | $ 44.95 |
| How to Best and Most Profitably Publish Your Book (3) | 44.95 |
| How to Create, Share, and Preserve Your Life Story (3) | 44.95 |
| How to Sell 75% of Your Travel Writing (2 hrs) | 29.95 |
| How to Publish Your Own Book / Earn $50,000 Profit (2) | 29.95 |
| Writing Comedy Greeting Cards That Sell! (2) | 29.95 |

| BURGETT AUDIO CASSETTE SINGLES | |
|---|---|
| (50-60 minutes) | |
| Producing and Selling Your Own Audio Cassette | $ 9.95 |
| Speakers: Using Your Book to Penetrate Your Niche Market | 9.95 |
| Speakers: How to Earn Happily Everafter With One Speech | 9.95 |
| Speakers: Generating Back-of-the-Room Product Sales | 9.95 |

| BURGETT REPORTS | |
|---|---|
| 100 Best U.S. Travel Newspaper Markets (annual) | $ 12 |
| 25 Professional Query and Cover Letters | 12 |

Some products are also available as electronic downloads, at reduced prices. Please check at www.super-second-life.com/cuproducts.htm

**Tax:** California orders, add 7.5% sales tax
**Shipping**: All orders, add $2.50 total

---

**Communication Unlimited**
P.O. Box 6405
Santa Maria, CA 93456
(800) 563-1454 / fax (805) 937-3035